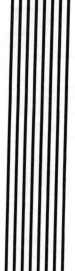

BURN THIS

BY
LANFORD WILSON

★

★

DRAMATISTS
PLAY SERVICE
INC.

For Peter, Sam, Lindsay, Tom, John,
David, Joan, Nancy, Ben, Frank again,
Lou again, another David, and especially for
another Tom, another John, and Jessica

This is dedicated to the ones I love

BURN THIS was produced on Broadway by James B. Freydberg, Stephen Graham, Susan Quint Gallin, Max Weitzenhoffer, Harold Reed and Maggie Lear, at the Plymouth Theatre, on October 14, 1987. It was directed by Marshall W. Mason; the set design was by John Lee Beatty; the costume design was by Laura Crow; the lighting design was by Dennis Parichy; the music was by Peter Kater; the fight direction was by Randy Kovitz; the dramaturg for the production was Jack Viertel; and the production stage manager was Mary Michele Miner. The cast was as follows:

ANNA..Joan Allen
BURTON...Jonathan Hogan
LARRY ....Lou Liberatore
PALE ....John Malkovich

BURN THIS received its premiere at the Mark Taper Forum (Gordon Davidson, Artistic Director) in Los Angeles, California, on January 22, 1987, with the same cast as appeared in the Broadway production. The production later moved to the 890 Theatre in New York City, produced by Circle Repertory Company, on February 18, 1987, and then to the Royal George Theatre in Chicago, Illinois, produced by the Steppenwolf Theatre Company, on September 13, 1987.

CHARACTERS

ANNA
BURTON
LARRY
PALE

BURN THIS

ACT ONE

The setting is a huge loft in a converted cast-iron building in lower Manhattan, New York City. Factory windows, a very large sloping skylight, a kitchen area, a sleeping loft, a hall to the bathroom and Larry's bedroom, and another door to Anna's bedroom. The place is sparsely furnished. There is an exercise barre on one mirrored wall and a dining area. There are pipes on the ceiling, and an old sprinkler system is still intact. There is new oak flooring; the walls are white; the only picture is a large framed dance poster. A fire escape runs across the entire upstage.

It is the sort of place that you would kill for or wouldn't be caught dead in.

The time is the present. It is six o'clock in the evening, mid-October. The sky has the least color left, one lamp has been turned on.

Anna is huddled on a sofa, smoking. She has a drink. She is thirty-two, very beautiful, tall and strong. A dancer. A buzzer sounds. A moment later it sounds again. She hears it this time and jumps. She looks at the buzzer. It sounds again. She gets up and goes to it.

ANNA.   Hello?
BURTON'S VOICE.   Hi, it's me. I just heard.
ANNA.   Uh, Burton, could we make it another.... *(Sighs, buzzes him in, opens the apartment door and leaves, going toward the bathroom. After a moment Burton comes in. He is tall, athletic, and rather good-looking. He has big feet and big hands that he admires, cracking his*

knuckles, stretching his neck and shoulders. He is a writer and very interested in his process. He is in a sweat suit.)

BURTON. Oh, God, darlin', I heard twenty minutes ago.

ANNA. Yeah, it's not been fun. I didn't know if I wanted to let you in. I think if I have someone to cry on, I'll fall apart completely.

BURTON. Oh, God, how'd it happen?

ANNA. Oh, he and Dom rented a boat — you know, a little motor-boat, and some yacht or something ran them down.

BURTON. Goddamn.

ANNA. They were in the middle of the bay — it was just getting dark. Freak accident. They were taking their things off the island. They could have ferried the damn car over, but I guess they thought a boat would be more of an adventure, I don't know. The assholes. I've just been so angry with him. I mean, if you don't swim, damnit! There was a huge picture of Robbie in the *Post.* I threw it out. BRILLIANT YOUNG DANCER DROWNS. That bit. They shipped Dom's body back to California.

BURTON. That's where his folks are? Oh, man. I was gonna run, I saw Kelly in the park, I just hopped in a cab. You went to the funeral?

ANNA. Go? God. Larry and I spent the best years of our lives at that funeral yesterday. And then I got shanghaied into spending the night with the family.

BURTON. Oh, God.

ANNA. Really. I've been smoking one of Robbie's cigarettes that he squirreled away. First cigarette I've had since college. I've for-got how to smoke. And drinking vodka. I feel like a piece of shit, I'm not very good company.

BURTON. No, come on. I just wish I'd been here for you.

ANNA. Who knew where to reach you?

BURTON. I called from the lodge Wednesday, that's the only phone we saw in a week.

ANNA. Yeah, I got the message. Thanks. The kid who took it is a major fan of yours.

BURTON. Of mine?

ANNA. He was impressed all to hell.

BURTON. Nobody knows who writes movies.

8

ANNA.   Sure they do. He's a sci-fi freak. He thinks you and ... somebody are the two best writers in the business.

BURTON.   Exactly. *(Larry enters holding groceries. He is twenty-seven, medium everything, very bright, gay.)*

LARRY.   When the hell did you get home? I've been calling all day.

ANNA.   I'm sorry, love, I turned the phone off.

LARRY.   *(To Burton.)* Now you show up.

BURTON.   Great timing, huh?

LARRY.   Where were you?

ANNA.   You don't want to know, really.

BURTON.   She got waylaid into spending the night with the family.

LARRY.   Oh, God.

ANNA.   Really. *(She refills her drink.)*

LARRY.   Vodka? Is that two?

ANNA.   I think three.

LARRY.   You're going to get sloppy. Not that it matters. What do you want? You want bright and cheery, nothing happened? You want quiet, leave me alone? Or maybe talk about it and cry? You know me. I'm always willing to drape the joint in crepe.

ANNA.   How are you?

LARRY.   Oh, who knows? Hi, beautiful. How was Canada?

BURTON.   Great. Cold. Snowy. Exhausting. How's the advertising business?

LARRY.   It sucks the big one.

ANNA.   Poor baby, everything got dumped on Larry. You were in Canada, I was in Houston. He had to go out there and identify Dom and Robbie, notify their families, get Robbie's suit down for the funeral. Had to buy a dress shirt and tie; Robbie didn't own one.

LARRY.   Yeah, it was a lot of laughs. She told you about the funeral?

BURTON.   I just walked in.

LARRY.   The single most depressing experience of my life.

ANNA.   Really. There was this great baroque maroon-and-gold casket with these ormolu geegaws all over it — angels and swags. Robbie would have hated it.

LARRY. It looked like a giant Spode soup tureen.

ANNA. Everything was wrong. The whole company's in Sacramento, so only about six of his friends were there. The eulogy was — the priest hadn't seen him in six years. His folks hadn't seen him in five, did you know that?

LARRY. Jesus.

ANNA. Well, have you ever heard him talk about his family?

LARRY. One brother, I think.

ANNA. Now we know why. *(To Burton.)* There's brothers and sisters, aunts and uncles for days. And none of them had seen him dance!

BURTON. You gotta be kidding.

ANNA. Never. Can you believe it? We couldn't believe it. Oh, God, it was a total nightmare.

LARRY. They had no idea who he was at all.

ANNA. I was the *girlfriend,* can you stand it?

BURTON. Oh, good Lord.

ANNA. It hadn't even crossed my mind. Of course, living with a woman, what else is it going to be?

BURTON. Yeah, but he was hardly living in a closet. I mean, interviews in *The Advocate.*

ANNA. Well, they obviously don't subscribe. Oh, God. Okay. Larry and I take the bus out there.

LARRY. The whole town is a combat zone.

ANNA. I don't know what industry it was built on, but it's not there anymore.

LARRY. In its heyday it couldn't have been much more than a place to leave.

ANNA. At the station we're met by a rented black Cadillac and either the sister or sister-in-law. Did you hear?

LARRY. Not a word.

ANNA. She spoke so softly; we asked three times and finally just pretended to hear. We get to the church —

LARRY. Everyone descended on Anna like a plague of grasshoppers.

ANNA. No joke, they just thrashed me. I'm chaff.

LARRY. She's rushed off to the first five rows, with the family.

ANNA. I said, I'm the grieving —

BURTON. You're the bereaved widow, of course.

ANNA. Some aunt patting my arm, everyone sobbing and beating their breasts. Most of them had never seen him in their lives, you understand. We get to the cemetery. I got the distinct feeling I was expected to throw myself across that hideous casket.

LARRY. Absolutely.

ANNA. I'd have given fifty dollars for a veil. *(Pause.)* I just kept thinking the three of us grew up in such different circumstances. I mean, what could I know about the world living in Highland Park? But, Lord, Robbie grew up in such — I looked for his teacher, I couldn't remember her name; I asked them, they'd never even heard of her.

BURTON. He probably had to sneak off to class.

ANNA. No, he did, literally, I knew that. I tried to tell them about the dance Robbie and I were working on and how important he was to me. With all that drive. Having a friend who was that good pushing you. They wouldn't let me talk about his dancing at all. I thought I could be truthful about something.

BURTON. I wanted to see it.

ANNA. Our dance?

LARRY. It was good.

ANNA. Yeah, even Larry liked it. No, it had no volume, it was too much like Charley's work, anyway. But even my mother keeps a scrapbook, and all she wants is grandchildren.

BURTON. Someone to take over the business.

ANNA. Listen, that's probably all I'm good for, anyway. And quick. Oh, Lord, tell us about Canada. Maybe it'll take my mind off myself.

LARRY. No joke, we've been like this for three days.

BURTON. Feel my thigh. Just her.

ANNA. Good Lord. It must have been beautiful, huh?

BURTON. Yeah, but more strange. Very strange things happen to you up there. Very disconcerting. Two days it's seventy something, we're skiing across this hilltop; we're stark naked, carrying our backpacks.

LARRY. That must have been scenic. *(He goes to his room.)*

BURTON. Oh sure. Next day it was ten degrees and snowing. But amazing country. Incredible skies. Some of the land looks like

11

the moon, all gouged out. Very heavy glacier activity. Very barren, very lonely. I missed you up there. I think I came up with a idea, though.

LARRY. *(Off.)* God knows we need it.

ANNA. That's great.

BURTON. Whole new thing, not a space flick. Whole different venue. Takes place in maybe Jasper, way up in northern Alberta in ... with the aurora and ... I don't know, about ten different things. This one's weird. Amazing things happen to your mind, you feel like you're all alone, or you're one with the ... something, or ... well ... we don't have to talk about it now.

ANNA. No, what? Something should come from this week.

BURTON. *(Getting juice from the fridge.)* It was like a vision I had while we were going along this ridge, like the top of the world — all this snow, this bright sun, you get into a kind of trance. And I saw this whole story, kind of a weird-ass love story —

ANNA. Burton, a love story?

BURTON. — or really more like a — what? The wives of the whalers or sailors, out to sea....

ANNA. The wives out to sea?

BURTON. No, you know. Oh, great. The men, for years on end and the wives waiting on their widow's walk, waiting, walking back and forth, watching the water, the waves coming in, the sun going down, and the men never coming home. Sort of their *heart*, or the men out there on the sea, their *heart*. Where's that love, or what is it, that power that allows those people to sustain that feeling? Through loss, through death. Is it less than the feelings we have? So they can humanly *cope?* Or is it more? I think they felt things in a much more profound way. There's some humongous mega-passion, something felt much deeper than we know. I don't know.

ANNA. I love it when you get an idea. You're so confused and enthusiastic.

BURTON. Am I?

ANNA. It's a good sign.

BURTON. It's there, it's just all fragmented. I had this book of Nordic tales, totally foreign from our stupid urban microcosm, all that crap.

ANNA. You never write urban microcosms anyway.

12

BURTON. Well, I know, thank God. But out there ... or the prairies, hell, the seas of grass, those huge distances, sod busters, no one within three thousand miles. What *sustains* those people? Out to sea, two or three years at a time, some of those whaling voyages; the fortitude of that kind of love. God.... But light. Subtle. Don't bang 'em over the head. I don't know. *(Pause.)* I don't think I can use it.

ANNA. Why not? It sounds terrific.

BURTON. No, it's all been done. It's not right. I'd write it, in shooting it'd all be degenerated into some goddamned gothic horror. The handsome sailor away at sea, the evil brother usurps the estate. Seen it a thousand times. Write a sod buster, they'd turn out *Little House on the Prairie. (Larry reenters.)*

ANNA. No, do it. I want to see it.

BURTON. No, that's just a phantom that haunts you up there. Everything is so good it makes you want to do something good, too. Or I just haven't got that thing yet ... how that environment impinges on the personalities, what that does to the women, the men ... the ... what?

LARRY. Robots.

BURTON. No robots. I love the space stuff, but on this one I'm looking for passions, faith, myths, love, derring-do, for godsake. Heroes and heroines.

LARRY. Senta throwing herself into the sea.

BURTON. Who's Senta?

LARRY. After the Dutchman sails away.

BURTON. I don't know it.

LARRY. *The Flying Dutchman.*

BURTON. I don't know *The Flying* fuckin' *Dutchman.*

ANNA. It's probably in your book of Nordic myths.

LARRY. Really. The Dutchman's this sailor who is like condemned to perdition unless he finds a girl who'll really love him. But he can come ashore only once every seven years to look for her.

BURTON. Why?

LARRY. You don't ask why in Wagner. So he goes to Norway and Senta falls in love with him, but she has this boyfriend hanging around and the Dutchman gets uptight and sails off again. And Senta throws herself into the ... fjord.

BURTON.   To prove she loved him.

LARRY.   To save him from perdition, to break the spell. The sea starts boiling, the Dutchman's ship sinks, all hell breaks loose.

ANNA.   Big finish.

BURTON.   I like the sea boiling, but I'm not that much of an opera queen.

LARRY.   I'm not an opera queen, Burton. I've seen opera queens, and believe me, I rank no higher than Lady-in-Waiting.

BURTON.   *(Looks at his wristwatch.)* Oh, Christ, I have to call Signer. I was supposed to have dinner with him tonight.

ANNA.   No, don't call it off, tell him the new idea.

BURTON.   What do you want to do?

ANNA.   I'm going to soak in a tub. Really. I've been in these clothes for two days. You go. Tell him about —

BURTON.   No, I'm not ready for him. I shouldn't even be talking about it at this stage. It's the same song every time I see him. God knows what I'd say. Met him once after he'd read a first draft; he's got this crushed look, he hands me the script, says, "What happened to the tiny Australian Bushman?" I still don't know what the fuck he was talking about.

LARRY.   Doesn't it just rip you to pieces what they do to your scripts? Did you see *Far Voyager*? After they got through with it?

BURTON.   I saw my bank account when they bought it.

LARRY.   You don't need money.

BURTON.   Tell me what I need.

LARRY.   You're rich as Croesus; you were born rich as Croesus.

BURTON.   Even Croesus needed money.

LARRY.   There was some beautiful writing in —

BURTON.   Beautiful writing? Is anathema to a movie. No, you can't get involved with it. You'd kill yourself. You can't worry what they're going to do to it. Start something else; take your four hundred thou and split.

LARRY.   It could have been a good movie if you'd —

BURTON.   It couldn't have been a good movie; there is no such thing as a good movie.

LARRY.   *Far Voyager* was wonderful before —

BURTON.   There are no good movies. *(To Anna.)* Did you coach him? *(To Larry.)* It can't happen. There cannot be a good movie.

14

When a good movie happens, which it might, on a roll of the dice, once in five years, it's like this total aberration, a freak of nature like the Grand Canyon, they're ashamed of it. They can't wait to remake it in another ten years and fuck it up the way it's supposed to be. Movies are some banker's speculation about how American adolescents want to see themselves that week. Period. They're produced by whores, written by whores, directed by —

LARRY.   Burton, you don't have to tell me about whores, you're talking to someone who works in advertising. Besides, I don't want to hear it. I think movies are gorgeous: "Who are you? Where did you come from? What do you want? It's me, isn't it? You've always wanted me. You want to have your filthy way with me in the hot desert sun. Ravage me like I've never been ravaged before." *Lust in the Dust.*

BURTON.   He memorized that?

LARRY.   Burton, you don't memorize. There are some things so true that they enter your soul as you hear them. You should be producing your own stuff, anyway; at least you wouldn't have done that Pit and the Pendulum scene in *Far Voyager.* Saved by forty midgets.

BURTON.   *Midgets?*

LARRY.   I thought you saw it.

BURTON.   No, I just wrote it; I couldn't sit through it. I heard what they did. The cave with the Vampire Queen — hanging upside down. No point in putting yourself through that kind of.... Midgets?

LARRY.   Munchkins. They did everything but sing "Ding Dong the Witch Is Dead."

BURTON.   Oh, Jesus. Well, Signer's short, he gets off on little people. I'm not as intrepid as Anna: quitting dance, trying to break into choreography....

ANNA.   Huh? Oh yeah, at this late date. By myself.

LARRY.   What, doll?

ANNA.   Nothing. What?

BURTON.   We're being insensitive and stupid.

ANNA.   No, I'm just out of it.

BURTON.   Would it be better if I left?

ANNA.   Actually, maybe so.

15

BURTON. Okay.

ANNA. Really. You should talk about Canada and I want to hear, but all I want to do right now is soak in a hot tub. What time's your dinner?

BURTON. I'll have to get some of this in the computer if I'm going to see him. I came over, I didn't know you'd still be here. You finished with Houston?

ANNA. You kidding? I've got to go back at noon for the reception tomorrow night. I didn't even pack, I just got on a plane. I don't suppose you have any desire to see Houston?

BURTON. Why not?

ANNA. No, I'm okay. I'm glad you're back.

BURTON. When we're not feeling so bad about this, we've got to get away. Go up to the Vineyard. Take a week off.

ANNA. Maybe it's time for us to just move up there permanently.

BURTON. I'd love it.

LARRY. Bye, beautiful.

BURTON. Yeah, sure. Take care of her. I gotta get gone. Call tomorrow.

ANNA. Bye-bye. *(Burton exits.)*

LARRY. I don't know why you don't just marry him and buy things.

ANNA. I'm glad he's come up with something. I think he was beginning to panic.

LARRY. I didn't visibly blanch when he said he gets two hundred thousand dollars for a first draft, did I?

ANNA. Well, he's got a name. You know. He's good. God, I'm as stiff as a board. I haven't exercised in two days. I'm completely out of touch with my body.

LARRY. When's your plane tomorrow?

ANNA. Noon. But I'm back the day after. Here for a week, then go to Seattle for no more than six days, and then that's it. No more teaching other companies Charley's dance.

LARRY. Concentrate on your own work.

ANNA. Whatever that is. I've already signed up for a class just to get Charley's damn movements out of my muscles. No lie; I could walk down the street, it's Charley walking down the street, it isn't me.

LARRY.   Should we have waited for you? After the funeral. Kelly had to work.

ANNA.   No, I should have come with you. God. Just as I think I'm out of there, some relatives drive me back to the house. The place is mobbed. I'm dragged through everybody eating and drinking and talking, to some little back bedroom, with all the aunts and cousins, with the women, right? Squashed into this room. His mother's on the bed with a washcloth on her forehead. I'm trying to tell them how I've got to get a bus back to civilization.

LARRY.   This is very moving, but I'm double-parked.

ANNA.   Exactly.

LARRY.   This is a *wake?*

ANNA.   I couldn't tell you *what* it was, Larry, I guess. In about eight seconds I know they have no idea that Robbie's gay.

LARRY.   I could have told you that.

ANNA.   They've never heard of Dom. God, I'm making up stories, I'm racking my brain for every interesting thing anyone I know has done to tell them Robbie did it. Wonderful workaholic Robbie, and I couldn't tell them a thing about him. It was all just so massively sad.

LARRY.   Oh, Lord.

ANNA.   It gets worse, it gets much worse. And they *never saw him dance!* I couldn't believe it. All the men are gorgeous, of course. They all look exactly like Robbie except in that kind of blue-collar, working-at-the-steel-mill kind of way, and *drink?* God, could they knock it back. So then it's midnight and the last bus has left at ten, which they knew, I'm sure, damn them, and I hadn't checked, like an idiot. So I have to spend the night in Robbie's little nephew's room in the attic. The little redhead, did you see him?

LARRY.   I didn't see him.

ANNA.   He's been collecting butterflies all day, and they're pinned around the room to the walls — a pin in each wing, right?

LARRY.   I'm not liking this little redheaded nephew.

ANNA.   Darling, wait. So. I get to sleep by about two, I've got them to promise to get me up at six-thirty for the seven-something bus. I wake up, it's not quite light, really; you can't see in the room much — but there's something *in* there.

LARRY. Oh, God.

ANNA. There's this intermittent soft flutter sound. I think what the hell is — Larry, the — oh, Lord, the walls are just pulsating. All those butterflies are alive. They're all beating their bodies against the walls — all around me. The kid's put them in alcohol; he thought he'd killed them, they'd only passed out.

LARRY. Oh, God.

ANNA. I started screaming hysterically. I got the bedsheet around me, ran down to the kitchen; I've never felt so naked in my life. Of course I was naked — a sheet wrapped around me. This glowering older brother had to go get my clothes, unpinned the butterflies, who knows if they lived. I got the whispering sister —

LARRY. What a family!

ANNA. — to drop me off at the bus station; they were glad to get rid of me. I was an hour and a half early, I didn't care. I drank about twenty cups of that vending-machine coffee. Black; the cream and sugar buttons didn't work. The bus-station attendant is ogling me. I'm so wired from the caffeine, if he'd said anything I'd have kneecapped him. There's these two bag ladies yelling at each other, apparently they're rivals. I fit right in.

LARRY. Oh, God. To wake up to those — I can just see them.

ANNA. Oh, Lord, I shrieked like a madwoman. They were glad to get rid of me.

LARRY. I was going to ask if you wanted coffee.

ANNA. No, I don't think that's going to do it.

LARRY. Not one of your better nights.

ANNA. Not one of my better nights. Not one of my better mornings.

LARRY. Jesus. What are we going to do about Robbie's mail?

ANNA. I guess save it. We have to bring Robbie's things down from the loft. Someone's coming over for them.

LARRY. He only had about two pairs of jeans and three sweat-shirts. A lot of shoes.

ANNA. Clothes didn't mean much to him.

LARRY. What did, except work and you and Dominic? In the room there's his futon, a candle, and a paperback of *Ancient Evenings.*

18

ANNA. *(Pause. She looks around.)* I left this place, went down to Houston ... I thought everything important to the future of dance was going to happen in this room. Oh, God. It's too early to go to bed.

LARRY. Go to bed now, you'd be wide awake at 2 A.M.

ANNA. Actually, you want to know the callous truth: if I were still dancing, I'd probably be brilliant tonight. *(Pause.)* How was work? Did they buy the idea?

LARRY. You have no notion of the stupidity involved in designing a Christmas card for a national company. Especially if it's Chrysler. Just for starters, there are a hundred seventy religions in America and only one of them believes in Santa Claus. Nothing religious; that would offend the non-believers. Reindeer are out — Santa Claus again. No snow; that would offend California and Florida. No evergreens, holly, pines — out of the question — no mistletoe, no bells. They said the only thing everyone believes in is the family and children. I said that was only going to offend homosexuals.

ANNA. Which didn't matter to them at all.

LARRY. No, I said it as a joke; they bought it.

ANNA. So what?

LARRY. They're still batting it around, but they're leaning toward a car. Which is tantamount to saying the only thing everyone believes in is the automobile.

ANNA. They're probably on to something there.

LARRY. Oh, I have no quarrel with that. A little plastic Chrysler that you can or not hang on your Christmas tree or Hanukkah bush that says *Season's Greetings from Chrysler Corp.* Made in Taiwan, appropriately. It's too complicated, production will get fucked completely, it's going to be late, and the cost is astronomical, but we won't have offended anyone. Except anyone with a modicum of taste. *(He looks at her, she stares off.)* What are you going to do about food? *(A very long pause.)* You wanta order in? Mexican? Pizza? Chinese? *(Pause.)* I haven't stopped thinking about it since it happened.

ANNA. I'm just so annoyed with myself, because all I can feel is anger. I was angry with Robbie and Dom for doing something that stupid; now I'm angry with his family. They just had no god-

19

damned right. He was my friend, damnit. I danced with him for three years. They didn't even know him.

LARRY.   They didn't do anything; there's no reason to be angry with them.

ANNA.   Well, I am. And there is. And they did. I mean, it's half sentimental horseshit, but damnit, they wouldn't leave me alone. I didn't even have a damn minute to say good-bye. I'll never forgive those bastards for that. *(Music up, the lights fade. After a moment of darkness there is a pounding on the apartment door.)*

PALE'S VOICE.   *(Offstage.)* Annie, hey, Annie — Just go fuck yourself, fella. Get laid, do you good. Annie. Hey. Come on. *(Anna turns on a light; she has quickly thrown on a Hapi coat. She looks through the peephole)* Come on. Come on. Jesus. *(She opens the door. Pale comes in. He is thirty-six, shorter than Burton, well built, and can be good-looking, but is certainly sexy. He wears a very good suit.)*

PALE.   Goddamn this fuckin' place, how can anybody live this shit city? I'm not doin' it, I'm not drivin' my car this goddamn sewer, every fuckin' time. Who are these assholes? Some bug-eyed, fat-lipped son of a bitch thinks he owns this fuckin' *space*. The city's got this *space* specially reserved for his private use. Twenty-five fuckin' minutes I'm driving around this garbage street; I pull up this space, I look back, this fuckin' baby-shit green Trans Am's on my ass going *beep-beep*. I get out, this fucker says that's my *space*. I showed him the fuckin' tire iron; I told the fucker, You want this space, you're gonna wake up tomorrow, find you slept in your fuckin' car. This ain't your space, you treasure your pop-up headlights, Ho-Jo. Am I right? That shit? There's no talkin' to shit like that.

ANNA.   I'm sorry, do I know you?

PALE.   How's that?

ANNA.   I mean, you're obviously some relation of Robbie's — you could be his double — but —

PALE.   Double, shit, with that fuckin' nose of his? Sure you know me — "Do I know you" — we met. I'm the one who saved you from the ferocious butterflies.

ANNA.   You have such a large family, I didn't really catch any *names*.

PALE.   Jimmy. I was listening to all that molasses you was pouring over Mom and all the cousins and neighbor bitches, I had to go take a shot of insulin.

ANNA.   I remember now, you're the older brother.

PALE.   Twelve years, so what? What's older? Older than what?

ANNA.   Older than Robbie.

PALE.   I said, didn't I? Twelve years. You hear me say that? He lived in this joint? I mean no personal disparagement of the neighborhood in which you have your domicile, honey, but this street's dying of crotch rot. The only thing save this part of the city, they burn it down. They call that a street out there? You could lose a Toyota some of those potholes. The people run your fuckin' city's got no respect for the property of the people livin' here. This is why people act the way they do, this shit. *(Beat.)* This has made me not as, you know — whatever — as I usually am. But I'm trying to parallel-park in the only fuckin' space a twenty-block radius, you don't crawl up my butthole in your shit-green Trans Am and go *beep-beep*, you know? *(Looking around.)* So'd you get the stuff together?

ANNA.   The what?

PALE.   The things, the things, the stuff, Robbie's shit.

ANNA.   Wait a minute, you've come for Robbie's things?

PALE.   Didn't I say?

ANNA.   It's been over a month. I called your mother. She gave me some numbers where I could reach you, but....

PALE.   Ya, sure. Listen, I don't want you bothering my family, okay? I don't like messages. The first one, you think, okay, fuck, I messed up. I'll take care of it, my fault, something came up, no problem. Then you get, you know, a couple of days, here's another fuckin' message. And it's like I heard you the first time, okay? Don't leave messages for me. I don't need the pool hall and the bar where I go and the auto-repair man on my back saying some bitch called and giving me a little piece of paper.

ANNA.   Saying what? Some bitch called? You were the one who was —

PALE.   That's the way he talks, what are we talkin'? A fuckin' bartender, what does he know? He's working some dark hole, listening to the dregs of the race vomit their life all over the bar

21

six nights; he's got a low opinion of humanity, okay? I don't like little pieces of paper. You put them in your pocket, you got six or eight little pieces of paper stuffed all over you, it ruins your clothes, you know? I don't read 'em. They're nothin' you don't already know. Somebody *wants* me, big fuckin' deal, take a number. I said I'd come, I'm here. A man would like to think people are gonna believe him. There's a certain satisfaction in being thought of as a man of your — There's something wrong with these shoes, my feet are in boiling water. *(He takes off one of his shoes.)* Look at that, oh man, I never had that.

ANNA.   Are they new?

PALE.   Yeah, first time I put them on. Don't worry about stinkin', I'm clean. They should invent a machine break in shoes — fuckin' killing the top of my foot. That's genuine lizard, two hundred forty-five bucks, fuckin' pinchin' everywhere. Jesus. *(He takes off the second shoe.)* You'd think a lizard's got to be supple, right? They got to move quick. Feel that. Steel plating. *(Walking.)* Oh man. *(Beat.)* What a fuckin' neighborhood. What a place to live.

ANNA.   Actually, we like it.

PALE.   Yeah, yeah, yeah, yeah, it's supposed to be arty, I know. It's quaint. Look at it — you should make automobile parts here; it's a fuckin' factory. *(Larry stands in his bedroom doorway in T-shirt and shorts.)* So who are you?

LARRY.   ... "Where did you come from? What do you want? It's me, isn't it? You've always wanted me. You want to have your filthy way with me in the hot desert sun. Ravage me like I've never been ravaged before." *(To Anna.)* Are you all right?

ANNA.   I'm fine. Larry, this is Jimmy, Robbie's brother.

LARRY.   I could tell.

PALE.   Your girlfriend is in very capable hands.

ANNA.   Larry's my other roommate.

PALE.   You're the replacement; that didn't take long — in one door, out the other.

LARRY.   The three of us got the place together.

PALE.   Didn't see you at the wake.

LARRY.   I wasn't invited. I'm going to bed, then. *(He exits.)*

ANNA.   Good night.

PALE.   "Good night," shit. Sleep tight. What am I gonna rip off the TV? He another dancer?

ANNA.   No. Listen, Jimmy, Robbie's things are in the basement. No way could you get them tonight without waking up the building. I've already called the Salvation Army, I hadn't been able to reach you.

PALE.   So what? What's this huge rush? They're on fire or something? Spontaneous combustion, something? *(There's a noise from the radiator.)* What's that?

ANNA.   The heat.

PALE.   Heat, yet. The fuckin' room's a oven, bake pizza here, they turn on some heat. *(He takes his jacket and tie off, pulls his shirttail out.)*

ANNA.   It's cold. It's the middle of winter.

PALE.   I got like a toaster oven I carry around with me in my belly someplace. I don't use heat. I sleep the windows open, no covers, I fuckin' hate things over me. Ray'll tell you: Here comes the dumb fuck Pale with the radiator up his ass. What time they turn it off?

ANNA.   Midnight. It comes back on at five.

PALE.   Five's ass, shit. It can't be no five. What'd I do with my watch?

ANNA.   Actually, I've got to get back to —

PALE.   Actually, would you just hold it a second, okay? *(Looking for his wristwatch.)* What'd I do with my — no, it's cool, I got it. *(He opens a window.)* Jesus, it's a fuckin' — you could pass out. How long did he live here?

ANNA.   About three years. He was a lot of fun.

PALE.   Yeah ... he was very light, a lotta guys are dark ... he was very light.

ANNA.   Yes he was. *(Pause.)* You want some coffee?

PALE.   Sure, whatta you got to drink?

ANNA.   Coffee.

PALE.   Sure. I'm not difficult.

ANNA.   You're Pale.

PALE.   V.S.O. Pale, that's me.

ANNA.   Robbie mentioned you.

PALE.   Yeah? He *mentioned* me? Well, I'm very mentionable.

ANNA. He didn't talk about his family much. You were the one he liked.

PALE. *(Looking out the window.)* That's the bay, huh, the river? Jesus. What a thing to look at. Oh, look, darling, they got tugboats pushin', like, these flatcars; like, five flatcars piled about a mile high with all this city garbage and shit. Who the fuck wants to look at that? You pay for a view of that? Maybe there's people find that fascinating, that's not what I call a view.

ANNA. Are you high?

PALE. How's that?

ANNA. Are you high? I mean, I know you've been drinking; I wondered if you were high, too.

PALE. Yeah, I did maybe a couple lines with Ray, it don't affect me.

ANNA. No, it doesn't affect you. *(She carries the coffee to the living area.)*

PALE. It don't affect me. This is the way I am, what you see, little girl. Straight or high. *(Larry stands in the doorway, only in his shorts.)* What is this, a slow strip act? *(Larry leaves.)* Jesus. Little girls your age don't have roommates, you know? This is not just me, this is prevailing opinion, here. *(He's looking out the window.)*

ANNA. I have a problem with prevailing opinions.

PALE. I could tell.

ANNA. They're putting up that building; it's going to block about half our view.

PALE. No, I'm trying to see where I parked my car. That jerkoff. People aren't human, you ever notice that? This bar tonight, Ray, you know?

ANNA. No.

PALE. Ray, Ray, Ray.

ANNA. No, I don't know him.

PALE. You may not know him. That didn't stop you asking him to write out your number on a piece of paper, give it to me; it didn't stop —

ANNA. Fine, Ray, fine, what about him?

PALE. Boy. So what? You dance here?

ANNA. Robbie and I used it as a studio, yes.

PALE. That's why you got no furniture, no curtains; you'll fall down over 'em, somethin'.

ANNA.   Actually, we've tried to keep it as spare as possible.

PALE.   This ain't spare. This is a empty fuckin' warehouse. *(He has found a bottle of brandy and pours himself a drink.)*

ANNA.   That's not V.S.O.P.

PALE.   I can tell. I got one area of expertise: food and drink.

ANNA.   Very — Something — Old — Pale.

PALE.   "Special." Most people don't even know what that means. Very Special Old Pale. This ain't bad, though, this ain't rotgut.

ANNA.   Thank you.

PALE.   What? You think it's hot shit? It's okay. It's no better than Rémy. I'd come in, I'd say Very Special Old Pale up, about the third time Ray says, Hey, Pale, on me.

ANNA.   This was when?

PALE.   When; shit, who knows? Ten, fifteen years. So you dance, too.

ANNA.   I did, I've taken off for a while.

PALE.   Couldn't stick it.

ANNA.   I decided it might be interesting to have a personal life.

PALE.   So. You got too good.

ANNA.   No, Robbie thought he saw a choreographer in me.

PALE.   So what do they do?

ANNA.   Choreographers? They make the dance. You have bodies, space, sculptural mass, distance relationships; if they're lucky, they might even discover they have something to say —

PALE.   So, you like it?

ANNA.   It's an interesting challenge. Well, it's becoming kind of an obsession.

PALE.   So you like it.

ANNA.   Uh, possibly. Look, if you wanted to come back seven, seven-thirty, we could go down to the basement and get —

PALE.   Seven-thirty I'm long outta here. No good. I'm a worker. Part of this country's great working force.

ANNA.   What do you do?

PALE.   Who me? Whatta I do?

ANNA.   It doesn't matter.

PALE.   I do anything. On call. Twenty-four hours a day and night. We never close. I deliver. Water. I'm a water deliverer. For fires. I put out fires. I'm a relief pitcher. Like Sparky Lyle.

ANNA. For whom?

PALE. Anybody needs relieving. I'm a roving fireman. Very healthy occupation. I'm puttin' out somebody else's fire. I'm puttin' out my own. *Quid pro* — something; symbiosis. Or sometimes you just let it burn. *(Pause.)*

ANNA. What did you do to your hand?

PALE. No, this bar tonight, Ray, you know?

ANNA. Good ol' Ray, sure. I mean, we've only talked on the phone.

PALE. There was this character runnin' off at the mouth; I told him I'm gonna push his face in, he don't shut up. Now, this should be a fairly obvious statement, right? But this dipshit starts trying to explain to me what he's been saying *ad nauseam* all night, like there was some subtle gradation of thought that was gonna make it all right that he was mouthing this horseshit. So when I'm forced to bust the son of a bitch, he's down on the floor, he's dripping blood from a split lip, he's testing a loose tooth, and that fucker is *still talking*. Now, some people might think that this was the problem of this guy, he's got this motor going, he's not privy to where the shutoff valve is. But I gotta come to the conclusion that I'm weird. 'Cause I try to communicate with these jerkoffs in what is *essentially* the mother tongue, but no one is picking me up; they're not reading me. There's some mystery here. Okay, sometimes they're just on a rap. I respect rap. You're not supposed to be listening. You can read the paper, watch TV, eat pistachios, I'm not talking that. I'm talking these jerkoffs think you're listening. You said the choreographer organizes what? Sculptured space? What is that?

ANNA. Oh, God. I'm sorry — What did you say? I'm sorry.

PALE. Now, see, that I can't take. I can't stand that.

ANNA. I'm sorry, really, but —

PALE. Well, see, fine, you got these little social phrases and politenesses — all they show me is this — like — giganticness of unconcern with your "I'm sorrys," man. The fuckin' world is going down the fuckin' toilet on "I'm sorrys." I'm sorry is this roll of toilet paper — they're growing whole forests, for people to wipe their asses on with their "I'm sorrys." Be a tree. For one day. And know that that tree over there is gonna be maybe music paper, the

26

Boss is gonna make forty million writin' some poor-slob-can't-get-work song on. This tree is gonna be ten-dollar bills, get passed around, buy things, *mean something*, hear stories; we got sketch pads and fuckin' "I don't love you anymore" letters pinned to some creep's pillow — something of *import*. Headlines, box scores, some great book or movie script — Jack Nicholson's gonna mark you all up, say whatever he wishes to, anyway, out in some fuckin' desert, you're supposed to be his *text*, he's gonna lay out this line of coke on you — Tree over there is gonna be in some four-star restaurant, they're gonna call him parchment, bake pompano in him. And you're stuck in the ground, you can't go nowhere, all you know is some fuckin' junkie's gonna wipe his ass and flush you down the East River. Go floating out past the Statue of Liberty all limp and covered with shit, get tangled up in some Saudi Arabian oil tanker's fuckin' propellers — you got maybe three hundred years before you drift down to Brazil somewhere and get a chance to be maybe a coffee bush. "I'm sorrys" are fuck, man. *(Pause.)* How long did he live here?

ANNA.   Three years. Did you know he was studying, Pale?

PALE.   Robbie? Didn't do much better than me. I was popular, you know. I don't think he wasn't so popular.

ANNA.   Dance, I mean. Did you know he wanted to be a dancer?

PALE.   Shit. I don't know. Whatta I know? He was seven, I was outta there. Who knew him? I didn't know him.

ANNA.   Actually, I was thinking that.

PALE.   Oh, beautiful, I love that. You're gonna be a cunt like everybody else? "You didn't really know him, Pale." *Deeply*, you gotta say. Did you know him deeply, honey? He know you deeply? You guys get deep together? 'Cause neither of you strikes me as the type.

ANNA.   Fine.

PALE.   What the fuck does that mean, "fine"?

ANNA.   It means I'm tired, it's five-thirty in the morning; if you don't want to talk about him, I certainly don't. You're completely closed; you knew him, I didn't. You don't want to hear what I have to say, fine. It means fine.

PALE.   What? I don't have feelings? I'm not capable of having a talk here?

ANNA.   There's no doubt in my mind that you have completely mastered half the art of conversation. *(Pale whistles.)* I'm tired. I'm sorry. I miss him. You remind me of him.

PALE.   Shit.

ANNA.   Completely aside from any familial resemblance, just having his brother here reminds me. At the — whatever that wake was after the funeral — it was obvious none of your family knew anything about him. Had you seen him dance? *(Pale shakes his head.)* Well, see, that's impossible for me to understand.

PALE.   Anybody good as he was, you said. He was good?

ANNA.   Yes.

PALE.   Well, see, that shows what the experts know. You saw him and say he was good. I didn't even see him, I know he was shit.

ANNA.   Pale, I can't stay up till the people in the building wake up, I have a class at nine, I have to get some rest.

PALE.   You teach?

ANNA.   What? No, a class I'm taking. I teach too, but this is a class. Then I come back here and work till six, so I've got a long day.... *(Pause.)* What?

PALE.   Awww, shit. *(Pause. He stifles a sob.)* Fuckin' ... drinkin' and thinkin', man, worse than drinkin' and drivin'. Drinkin' and thinkin'. Aw shit. He wasn't dark, you know, like....

ANNA.   *(Pause.)* He worked really hard.

PALE.   Awww, Jesus ... feed the fish, man ... Jesus. *(He sobs enormously and long, she goes to him, he moves away. She touches his shoulder.)*

ANNA.   I know.

PALE.   Come on, don't mess with me. I don't like being messed with. My heart hurts, I think I'm dying. I think I'm havin' — like — a heart attack. I messed up my stomach, I think I ate somethin'. *(Sobs again.)* I don't do this, this ain't me. *(He gets up, walks around.)* Aww shit. I'm trying to imagine him here.

ANNA.   His room was up in the loft.

PALE.   Yeah? What'd you do, you guys eat here; you have — like — parties, that shit?

ANNA.   Sometimes. When we were all home, which wasn't often enough, we'd trade around. We're all pretty good cooks. Robbie was really the best.

PALE.   Robbie cook?

ANNA.   He was working his way through *The Cuisine of Southern Italy.* Cookbook ... Dom ... someone gave him for Christmas.

PALE.   Shit. Fuckin' Christmas parties. Presents and that shit. Look out! Ribbons! I fuckin' hate that crap.

ANNA.   What do you like, Pale?

PALE.   I like a lot of things. You want bullshit, you want to know what turns me on?

ANNA.   Nothing. That's fine. I can imagine.

PALE.   Yeah, well, I don't like being imagined. I like the ocean. That hurricane. I stayed on the pier — hanging on to this fuckin' pipe railing, wind blowin' so hard you couldn't breathe. Couldn't open my hands the next day. Try to get excited over some fuckin' roller coaster, some loop-the-loop after that. I like those gigantic, citywide fires — like Passaic, wherever; fuckin' Jersey's burnin' down three times a week. Good riddance. Avalanches! Whole villages wiped out. Somethin' that can — like — amaze you. People don't want to hear that shit, they want — like you should get turned on by some crap — you know, Häagen-Dazs ice cream, "I like everyone to be nice." That shit. Chicks or somethin'. Gettin' laid's okay. A really hot shower's good. Clean underwear, smells like Downy softener. *(Beat.)* So you guys all cook for each other. Sittin' here, makin' polite conversation about the state of the world and shit.

ANNA.   Dancers mainly talk about dance.

PALE.   Man, I'm fuckin' up my pants all fucked up.

ANNA.   That's a nice suit.

PALE.   Yeah, I'm a dresser. I keep myself neat. I'm fuckin' up the back of my pants, gettin' all fucked up. Fuckin' linen. Half linen, half wool — fuckin' useless. I could've been the dancer. Who needs it? Our old man, when we was kids, music all over the place. You couldn't hear yourself think. Vivaldi, Puccini, we all knew all that crap, Shostakovich. I've done — like — whole symphonies, amazed people, natural talent, totally original shit, like in the shower. I don't sing Hall & Oates, I compose — like — these tone poems, concertos and shit — huge big orchestrations, use like two orchestras.

ANNA. Do you read music?

PALE. What for? Nobody does that shit. I get going some symphony, these like giant themes come to me, these like world-shaking changes in tempo and these great huge melodies, these incredible variations, man. Get like the whole fuckin' war in it. *(He stops, bends over.)* My heart's killing me. My throat's hurtin', burnin', man. What a fuckin' night. Bust up my hand on that fucker's tooth. *(He looks out the window. Pause.)* Half my fuckin' adult life, I swear to Christ, has been spent looking for a place to park. *(Beat. He looks at her.)* What are you wearin' that thing?

ANNA. I keep hoping I'll have a chance to go back to bed and get my rest.

PALE. Sure. Don't worry about rest, we'll all get our rest. Whatta you call that thing?

ANNA. It's called a Hapi coat.

PALE. That's somethin' to wear, you do your Hapi? The Indians wear that, the Hopis?

ANNA. I got it in Japan.

PALE. Those Orientals are short, it might give them better cover.

ANNA. I just grabbed something. *(Pause. He looks at her, looks around the room. Back to her.)*

PALE. So the three of you lived here. You and the two faggots.

ANNA. *(A long stunned pause.)* We were all very good friends.

PALE. Tellin' Mom and Aunt Ida and all the neighborhood bitches how you and Robbie did things, horseback, and the races and shit. Said everything except your little boy was a real hot fuck.

ANNA. *(Pause.)* It was very humiliating. They didn't know; it wasn't my place to tell them.

PALE. They know, they just don't know.

ANNA. Well, whatever. I didn't feel it was my place.

PALE. *(Banging on the sofa.)* Fuckin' fruit. Fuck! Fuck! Fuck! Fuck! Fuck! Bastard! Taking his fuckin' little Greek boyfriend out to the island, talking about him in the paper, on that TV thing. "You dance real good." "Well, I get a lot of help from my friend Dominic." Suckin' my dick for me, whatever the fuck they do.

ANNA. Don't you know? I thought you'd know. They have anal intercourse, take turns having oral —

30

PALE. HEY! HEY! People *see* those programs! On TV, Channel Q, whatever, don't matter. People see that. People say, I saw your queer brother on the TV with his boyfriend. People the family works for. That crap. He live here, too? Dominic?

ANNA. He spent about half the time here. We'd been trying to get him to move in, there's plenty of room. Dom was great, you'd have liked him. It's very different here without them.

PALE. I'm just trying to get a picture —

ANNA. Well, don't bother if you didn't give a damn for him; it's a little late to cry now.

PALE. — Robbie cookin', Dominic serving wine, you lighting candles. The fruit in there running around without his clothes on. *What do you know what I feel?* I got my hand bleeding again. Fuckin' myself into little pieces here. I got to wear this look like a fuckin' bum. *(He bends over, starts to cry, stifles it.)* Shit, man; shit, man. Awww shit. *(Taking off his pants.)* I can't get fucked up; you go get your rest, you're worried about rest. I can't fuckin' stand up; I sit down, I'm gonna cry. Come undone. I got to wear these tomorrow — *(Presses them on table)* I can't fuck myself.

ANNA. *(Overlapping.)* Jimmy, for godsake. Jimmy. If you're worried, I can press them in the morning. Seven o'clock we can go down to the basement. Listen, if you're very quiet, we can sneak down now. We'll take the stairs, 'cause the elevator — Jimmy. Jimmy. *(He has crawled onto the sofa and completely covered himself with an afghan, head and all. His body is racked with crying. Anna looks at him for a moment. She finishes the last of her coffee. What the hell — finishes his brandy as well. Sits on the sofa by him.)* I know. I miss him like hell. I go to the studio, I think I see him ten times a day. Someone dressed like him, or walking like him. Then I remember he's gone, and it's all that loss all over again. I know.

PALE. *(He has poked his head from the afghan.)* He was always ... very.... *(Gestures light.)*

ANNA. I know. He worked harder than anyone I've ever known.

PALE. *(Looks around.)* Where's my....

ANNA. I drank it.

PALE. I'm gonna have to have another. *(She gets up.)* I'll get it.

ANNA. That's okay, you got the last one.

PALE. I'll send you a fuckin' case.

ANNA. It's fine, Jimmy. Just — what? Cool it, okay?

PALE. Jimmy you're callin' me. I like that. Nobody calls me that. Fuckin' place, man. Fuckin' haunted.

ANNA. Yes, it is. So's the studio. So's the streets around the neighborhood. *(Sitting on the sofa.)* So's the whole island of Manhattan.

PALE. So's Jersey. *(Pause.)* I'm gonna be sick here.

ANNA. The brandy doesn't help.

PALE. No, it's good for it. You don't do nothing to your hair? It's just like that?

ANNA. It costs a fortune. *(Pause.)* Oh, God.

PALE. You're done in, huh?

ANNA. No, I'm up. I'm an early riser, anyway. Not usually this early, but.... No, I'm just ... blue. Remember that? When people used to feel blue? I'm feeling blue.

PALE. Me too. *(Not looking at her breasts or touching them.)* You almost got no tits at all, you know?

ANNA. I know. Thanks.

PALE. No, that's beautiful. That's very provocative. Guy wants to look, see just how much there is. Tits are very deceptive things. *(Pause. Rubs his chin on the top of her head. Sings very softly, very slowly from "St. Louis Blues.")* "Just as blue as I can be ... that gal got a heart like a rock cast in the sea...."*

ANNA. You're burning up.

PALE. That's just the toaster oven. Always like that.

ANNA. You're not sick, you don't have a fever?

PALE. Normal temperature about a hundred and ten. Aww, man, I'm so fucked. My gut aches, my balls are hurtin', they're gonna take stitches on my heart; I'm fuckin' *grievin'* here and you're givin' me a hard-on. Come on, don't go away from me — everybody's fuckin' flyin' South, man ... like I was the.... aw shit, man. I'm gonna cry all over your hair. *(He does cry in her hair.)*

ANNA. What, Jimmy?

PALE. Come on, don't look at me.

ANNA. Jimmy, stop. Enough already, don't; you're gonna hurt yourself or something.

PALE. Good. Good. Don't look.

ANNA. I was very angry at the funeral. I thought I hadn't had

*See Special Note on Songs and Recordings on copyright page.

a chance to have a moment, but Larry and I went back to the cemetery a couple of days after and we cried the whole day; but don't break your heart. You know? *(Kisses him lightly.)* Jimmy?

PALE. You went back?

ANNA. Larry and I.

PALE. Come on. You make me upset.

ANNA. You're making yourself upset.

PALE. No, the other way. I'm getting all riled here. I got no place for it. I got like a traffic jam here. *(Kisses her lightly.)* You okay?

ANNA. I'm fine.

PALE. I'm like fallin' outta the airplane here. *(Pause.)* You always smell like that?

ANNA. Shampoo.

PALE. My shampoo don't make me smell like that. Let's just start up the engines real slow here ... maybe go halfway to the city and stop for somethin' to eat.... You talk to me, okay?... You're gonna find out there's times ... I'm a real good listener. *(Music up, fade to black. After a few moments the lights come back up. Very early morning. Sunny. Larry enters from outside.)*

LARRY. *(Entering yelling.)* He might have told me I was going to have to load his car by myself. I adore manual labor at 6:50 A.M. God, I thought he was going to help.

ANNA. *(Coming in from the bedroom.)* He's been on the phone.

LARRY. Where the hell is he?

ANNA. Taking a shower.

LARRY. Any great tone poems come out of there yet?

ANNA. Not a peep.

LARRY. He's probably going to be another big bruiser with a bad back.

ANNA. No, I don't think so.

LARRY. One is not allowed to be smug just because one got laid. *(At Pale's jacket and pants, holds up a pistol.)* Please note.

ANNA. Don't touch it. I saw.

LARRY. Robbie's address book just happened to fall out of one of the boxes and into my pocket. "Pale: 17 Oak Street, Montclair, New Jersey." Phone number at home, phone number at work.

ANNA. What would you say to an omelette?

LARRY.   Uh ... *Bonjour, omelette.* I'm exhausted, of course; my eyes did not close. I had one hand on the phone and the other with a finger poised to dial 911. Actually, that's not true. With all the music coming out of this room, I abused myself terribly. *(Pale enters, fresh shirt and tie, puts on pants, steps into shoes while dialing.)* You always carry a spare shirt in the car?

PALE.   What? Yeah. *(On phone.)* Joe. Pale. Fifteen minutes. You just be damn sure you hold them. Just don't fuck me. Fifteen minutes. You got what? No, no, I can't use it. No. I'm leavin' now. *(Hangs up.)* More fuckin' trouble than my old lady.

LARRY.   Than your old what?

PALE.   What, you think I'm weird or something? Sure I got an old lady. Two kids, perfect family. *(Hands Anna his opened wallet.)* Boy and girl.

ANNA.   Won't she be curious where you spent the night?

PALE.   Naw, she trusts me; they're down in Coral Gables. She knows I'm cool. I never cheated on her once.

ANNA.   *(Handing him the wallet.)* They're beautiful.

PALE.   You get that crap in the car?

LARRY.   All loaded.

ANNA.   You want coffee? Maybe an omelette?

PALE.   Got no time. Don't use food in the morning. I can't drink coffee, burn your guts out. You got my keys? cigarette lighter?

LARRY.   On the counter. That's a great-looking car.

PALE.   Fuckin' pain in the ass, too. Okay, people, I'm out of here. *(He exits.)*

LARRY.   He's one of those people you know right away isn't going to say, "Have a nice day." So, is he utterly fantastic in the sack?

ANNA.   Uh ... quite interesting.

LARRY.   *(Sings.)* "Just as blue as I can be...."*

ANNA.   *(Glaring at him.)* How much did you hear?

LARRY.   I'm trying to remember.... No, I don't think I missed anything.

ANNA.   Sorry. Very bad form. It was all very — oh, what the hell. The bird-with-the-broken-wing syndrome.

LARRY.   You bring the poor little bird home, doll. You make a splint for its poor little wing. You feed the little bugger chicken

---

*See Special Note on Songs and Recordings on copyright page.

34

soup if you must. You don't, however, fuck it. *(He has been dialing the phone.)* Hello. Is Pale there?

ANNA.   You're not.

LARRY.   Eleven? What exactly is his position there? Manager. And this is the ... Da Signate Ristorante.

ANNA.   Oh no. Hang up.

LARRY.   Thank you. No, no message, he hates them. *Grazie. (Hangs up.)* Manages a restaurant. I love it.

ANNA.   Oh, God. He's a relief pitcher. Yeah, of sangría.

LARRY.   I've been there; it's celebrity city, two stars or something.

ANNA.   Well, he said he worked hard.

LARRY.   They do, too. Tom managed a restaurant in the Village for two years. He had to be down at the Fulton Fish Market at six in the morning or it was gone.

ANNA.   That's probably who he was calling.

LARRY.   "This is Pale, hold my scrod." I love it. With a gun, though?

ANNA.   If he makes the deposits at night.

LARRY.   I think you're very wise. One of those people it'd be impossible to get rid of any other way. *(Phone rings.)* That's Burton to tell you how many laps he made around the reservoir.

ANNA.   Seven o'clock on the nose.

LARRY.   *(On the phone.)* Hello, beautiful. I get up early sometimes. Part of my charming unpredictability. Actually, I was up with Anna all night. No, nothing serious. Said she felt like she had a terrible weight on her stomach.... *(Looking at her.)* I just hope she doesn't come down with something. I'm sure she'd love to, only nothing too physical, she looks exhausted.

ANNA.   *(Taking the phone.)* Hi, Burt. No, I'm fine, never better.

LARRY.   Rub it in.

ANNA. What's to see? Yeah, that'd be fun. Or the other one. No, I don't think so. I've just got no interest in it. The what? *(Covers the phone.)* Would you shut up? *(To Burton.)* That's good, then. Okay, sevenish. *(Hangs up the phone.)*	LARRY. *(Sings.)* "Just as blue as I can be ... that Pale got a heart like a rock cast in the sea...."*

*See Special Note on Songs and Recordings on copyright page.

LARRY.   Slut.

ANNA.   Oh, God. He wants to go out tonight.

LARRY.   And of course, out of abject guilt, you said sure. You could always have said, I couldn't possibly, I was fucked blind last night.

ANNA.   Go to hell.

LARRY.   Please note how contact with your restaurateur has eroded our speech. We're just at the age where we pick that sort of thing up.

ANNA.   I'm going back to bed.

LARRY.   You'll miss class and you've got work to do.

ANNA.   I'll take a shower and think about it.

LARRY.   What would you say to a waffle?

ANNA.   Get lost, waffle. Get thee behind me. Which is exactly where it would go. *(She starts for the bathroom. Sings.)* "That man got a heart ... like a rock cast in the sea...."* *(She stops with a shock, turns to look at Larry. Pause. Larry stands looking at her. He sings softly to her.)*

LARRY.   "Oh ... oh ... oh ... I'm on fire ..."** *(Music up, the lights fade.)*

*See Special Note on Songs and Recordings on copyright page.
**See Special Note on Music on copyright page.

ACT TWO

Late New Year's Eve. 2 A.M. Anna is in a gown, Burton in a tux. Anna has a script in her hands. She finishes reading it.

BURTON. That's as far as I've got.

ANNA. Oh, I like it. It's so sad. God.

BURTON. Sad? I thought they were having fun.

ANNA. Oh no, sure. But underneath all that, God, they're so lonely.

BURTON. Yeah, I know, but I don't want to think about that part or I won't be able to do it. Aw, to hell with it, anyway. I want something larger than life. Those people are smaller than life.

ANNA. They're very real, and I think it's exciting. And you have your space. Only it's distance between people rather than distance between places.

BURTON. No, give me kinky or quirky or sadistic — Where's the pain? Where's the joy? Where's the ebullience?

ANNA. It's there. Everything doesn't have to be epic.

BURTON. Yes! Yes! Not in treatment, but at least in feeling. Reach! Reach for something! God! Reach for the sun! Go for it!...

ANNA. I don't think I've been sober on New Year's Eve before in my life.

BURTON. Not necessarily recommended.

ANNA. You were doing all that coke.

BURTON. Not the same thing.

ANNA. I've missed you. How was your family?

BURTON. Rich, self-satisfied, alcoholically comatose, boring. *(Pause.)* Before we get off the subject, you really did like it?

ANNA. I really do. That other character is Larry, isn't he?

BURTON. Larry? No. Well, you know. Some him, some — no more than ninety percent. How's it been going here?

ANNA.   I'm working like a dog. I almost feel as if I've finally burst my chrysalis after thirty years of incubation. That's the wrong word.

BURTON.   Metamorphosis.

ANNA.   The day after you left, Fred asked me to do a piece with a company he's putting together.

BURTON.   All right!

ANNA.   It's kinda exciting, really. Guaranteed coverage, maybe a little more — what? — political than I'd like — three new woman choreographers. Twelve minutes or so each. The first half of a new program he's working on. God. He pays the rent, the advertising. Overall theme, very loosely, is love. Mother love, which God knows I know nothing about — yet. And then something else, and he wants me to do the *pas de deux*. Two couples, not one.

BURTON.   *Pas de quatre.*

ANNA.   He's got four great kids for me to work with. I try things out here and work with them at Fred's studio. I think it'd be fair to say it's not going well. I'm beginning to think that as an artist I have absolutely no life experience to draw from. Or else I'm just too chicken to let anyone see what I really am.

BURTON.   What you need is to do a little research on this love stuff. Tonight.

ANNA.   Well, if I'm going to pretend to know anything about it....

BURTON.   It might get a little X-rated.

ANNA.   A *pas de quatre* for Fred, that's absolutely *de rigueur*.

BURTON.   What's your schedule tomorrow?

ANNA.   Totally clean slate.

BURTON.   Me too.

ANNA.   Actually, I planned ahead. You've been ambushed. *(She takes a bottle of champagne from the fridge.)* I even bought a new flute. Have you ever seen anything that beautiful in your life? Listen. *(She rings the glass lightly.)* Do you believe that?

BURTON.   What's the difference between a flute and a glass?

ANNA.   About fifty bucks. Would it be unbearably provocative if I slipped into something less formal?

BURTON.   Unbearably, without doubt. Do it.

ANNA.   Undo.

BURTON.   Whatever happened to zippers? There's nothing so beautiful as the sound of a long zipper down a woman's back.

ANNA.   I'll remember.

BURTON.   Also, I need the practice. It's been a while, you know.

ANNA.   You have to give the story another week — I want to see where it goes. *(Exits into the bedroom.)*

BURTON.   *(Raising his voice slightly.)* No, you were saying you were chicken; I think that's what's happening. I don't want to know. I need to get out of the city or something — do something — shake things up. You sure you don't want to give up this loft and move in my place?

ANNA.   *(Offstage.)* Never. You want to live with me, you move in here.

BURTON.   Maybe I should. Have kids or something.

ANNA.   *(Offstage.)* At least then I could do the piece on mother love. That's something I haven't thought about much. Or every time I did, I pushed it out of my mind. But now — I don't know. I think my body chemistry is changing, or maybe I just have time to think of things like that now. I can feel a kind of anxiety or panic creeping up on me. The sound of the biological clock or something. Which is probably only another way of avoiding work. Any excuse.

BURTON.   I know the feeling. Every time I start to work on the love story I swiftly segue into droid-busting on Barsoom. I've been working on a kind of extension of the *Far Voyager* story —

ANNA.   *(Offstage.)* Do the other one.

BURTON.   The space stuff's more fun. The other one isn't fun. I'm talking about myself again! I don't believe it. It's unconscious. *(Anna comes back into the room in full dressing gown.)* That's gorgeous. *(He holds her a moment. They sit and start to toast. There is a noise at the door.)* What the hell?

ANNA.   What time is it? It's Harrison across the hall, or maybe Larry coming home.

BURTON.   Oh, God, let it be Harrison across the hall. I thought Larry wasn't due back till tomorrow.

ANNA.   I think tonight.

BURTON.   Well, fuck.

ANNA.   Well, later at least.

LARRY.   (*Enters carrying three huge suitcases. He drops them and staggers across the room, collapsing on the sofa.*) I'm dying. Oh, God. Ask me where I was when we rang in the New Year. My arms are dead, they're falling off.

ANNA.   Where were you when we rang in the New Year?

LARRY.   Circling about ten thousand feet over Queens. And we had been for forty-five minutes. And we continued to for another hour. I was praying we would crash and burn. There was not a happy person on the plane. Everyone was going to a party. Nobody made it. Midnight came and went, nobody said a word. We just glared at each other. The last hour there wasn't a stewardess in sight, they were all up in the cabin with the pilot; we landed, one of them was visibly drunk.

BURTON.   I thought you like to travel; you liked meeting people.

LARRY.   The man next to me, I strongly suspect, was either Jerry Falwell himself or a member of the Supreme Court. Total Nazi. After half an hour of theories on the Sanctity of the Home and the American Family as the Last Bastion of Christian Liberty (whatever the hell that is) I said, "Well, being a cocksucker, of course, I disagree with everything you've said." I was so angry I didn't even get off on it. That's what going home does to me — I lose my protective sense of humor. My arms are falling off.

ANNA.   Happy New Year.

LARRY.   Fuck you both. What are you doing here? Why aren't you out partying?

ANNA.   It's two-thirty, we're back.

LARRY.   From where?

ANNA.   We went to a party. I liked it, didn't you?

BURTON.   Yeah, it was fun. Up in SoHo.

ANNA.   A bunch of the new young geniuses and starlets. I didn't know many of them. Burt can tell you.

BURTON.   Nice group. So how's beautiful Detroit?

LARRY.   Burton, "beautiful Detroit" is an oxymoron. Detroit is the South's revenge. You don't want to start your New Year with the story of the faggot's Christmas in Wales, believe me. (*He lights a cigarette.*)

ANNA.   When did you start smoking?

LARRY. How long have I been gone?

ANNA. You've got a dozen invitations to parties; hop in a cab, have some fun. They'll go on all night.

LARRY. Have you ever been to a gay New Year's Eve party? The suicide rate is higher than all of Scandinavia combined. My arms are falling off, my head hurts, I'm exhausted. For the first time in my life I have sympathy for Olga in *Three Sisters*.

ANNA. Go out. Meet someone.

LARRY. Anna, an Olympic gym team performing naked would not turn me on. The defensive front line of the Pittsburgh Steelers could rape me on the floor of the locker room, I'd bring them up on charges. If you're trying to ditch me, forget it. Go to Burton's. Oh, God. I have six nephews I'd never met before. And hope not to see again until they're sixteen. And two nieces. Both of my sisters *and* my brother's wife have turned into baby machines. What is happening to women? Ten years ago they were exciting entities; they're all turning into cows.

BURTON. We were just talking about that.

ANNA. I get more of an image of a brood sow. Flat out in the mud, with about ten piglets squealing around you, trying to nurse. Have you ever seen that? Their eyes rolled back in their heads? Lying back in the sun, in some other world.

LARRY. I hope you don't think you're making it attractive. They all wrote down their kids' birthdays so I'd be sure to send something. There's doomsday factor in our genes somewhere. Through the entire history of the species it's been the same story — the wrong people reproduce. *(Goes to Anna.)* Happy New Year. *(Kisses her lightly on the lips.)*

ANNA. Happy New Year.

LARRY. *(Goes to Burton, kisses him lightly on the lips.)* Happy New Year.

BURTON. Happy New Year, Uncle Larry.

LARRY. Burton — you're a black belt in karate —

BURTON. Brown.

LARRY. You teach judo at the "Y" —

BURTON. Akido.

LARRY. I don't care. One more crack and I'll rip your eyes out. Oh, God, when did you last see a grown man cry?

41

ANNA.   Un ... actually — when was it? The day after you left. I ran into an old friend of yours.

LARRY.   I have no old friends. If I do have, I won't after this trip, because I'm going to be unbearable for a month.

ANNA.   I think he was actually closer to Robbie than to you.

LARRY.   Oh, please. I loved him dearly, but all Robbie's friends talked about dance with that fanatical glazed look across their eyes that always — Closer, how? You don't mean he was crying in his V.S.O. cognac...?

ANNA.   I think that's the only thing he drinks.

LARRY.   And this was where...?

ANNA.   Midtown. Mid-morning. One drink. And I fled.

LARRY.   Drinking in the mid-morning. You *have* gone downhill without me.

ANNA.   I had coffee.

BURTON.   Who was this?

LARRY.   Just a Pale page from my checkered past. I don't think he came here more than once. Or I should say, I don't think he's *been* here more than once. Please note, my last cigarette. *(He stubs out the cigarette and puts the pack away.)* Did Anna tell you she's working on a dance for Fred?

BURTON.   Yeah, that's great.

ANNA.   Oh sure — scares the hell out of me.

LARRY.   I love it. I come home, she's dancing up a storm.

ANNA.   I was flying around here the other day. I flop down, I think that's great; then I thought, I wonder if I could get arrested for that?

LARRY.   In some states....

ANNA.   I think it's all getting a little too personal.

BURTON.   Good, it's supposed to be — Make it as personal as you can. Believe me, you can't imagine a feeling everyone hasn't had. Make it personal, tell the truth, and then write "Burn this" on it.

ANNA.   Burton, at least, has made a giant leap into the unknown.

BURTON.   Yeah, I've taken up skydiving.

ANNA.   He's started working on something real.

BURTON.   Naw, that's nothing, goes nowhere.

ANNA.   It takes place in the city, and is some kind of love story with real people, so, of course, he doesn't trust it.

BURTON.   I don't even know why I wrote it down. I was bored.

ANNA.   I think it's very hot.

LARRY.   So am I gonna see it?

ANNA.   Let him read it — it's only twenty pages.

BURTON.   No, it's nothing. Come on.

LARRY.   This is the Northern thing?

BURTON.   The what? Oh no ... I tried to do something on the Northern thing; it turned into this city thing.

ANNA.   We were about to toast the New Year.

LARRY.   *(Seeing the flute glasses.)* Where did those come from? They're gorgeous.

ANNA.   Baccarat. They were in the window.

LARRY.   How many?

ANNA.   Four. It did in my life savings.

LARRY.   I'm in love. I'm going to sleep with them.

ANNA.   Happy New Year. *(They all toast, say "Happy New Year," and drink.)* Oh, Lord. That makes you understand what they mean by champagne.

LARRY.   Home again, home again....

ANNA.   Jiggity-jig. *(A distant bell sounds.)*

BURTON.   Where the hell is there a bell at this hour?

LARRY.   I didn't imagine there was such a thing as a real bell anymore. I thought they were all recordings blasted over loud-speakers.

BURTON.   The first year I was in New York I had a job as a messenger. I took a package to this poet's loft —

ANNA.   Messenger?

BURTON.   I must have been eighteen.

ANNA.   God knows you didn't need the money.

BURTON.   I know, but I decided I should experience work — I forget why. Anyway, this poet was over on Fourth Avenue, across from the church there. And we got to talking. He asked me what I did and I said I was a writer; turned out he was a poet and I'd read some of his stuff, and he was impressed and I was impressed, and we had a drink and a joint and sat around — this is not a job that I kept for very long.

LARRY.   I can see that. Actually, I imagine he was trying to think of a way to get in your pants.

BURTON.   Oh, for godsake — why is it always that? Why does it always have to be that with you?

LARRY.   Burton, you're talking about a poet. Why does it always have to be that? Ask your priest; I didn't invent people. It's just always that. Anyway.

BURTON.   So anyway — the church bells started ringing. We were sitting in the open window, on a big window seat, right across the street from the bell tower, and he said, Poe, Edgar Allan Poe used to live in that apartment. And those bells were the bells, bells, bells, bells, bells, bells, bells.

ANNA.   Oh, God. The tintinnabulation. Where?

BURTON.   Fourth Avenue and about East Tenth. He got the apartment because of them.

ANNA.   Of course he did.

BURTON.   Actually, Larry — this'll give you a thrill — he *was* gay and I knew it, and it never crossed my mind he was anything but sincere. I really don't think he was trying to make me.

LARRY.   It's possible, Burton. In a different world. But who knows what world poets live in, so —

BURTON.   You want to know something? One time — you should know this — when I was twenty — two years later — I'd been here two years and a half. I was up around Columbia. I decided to walk down to the Village. I had to piss so bad — about Fifteenth Street and Eighth or Ninth Avenue — middle of the — say 1 A.M. — and I mean, it's cold. It'd started to snow, so everything was white. I pissed up alongside a doorway, I was feeling very high — on the night, nothing chemical — and this guy sidles up to me from nowhere — there wasn't another person on the street — and he says, "You live around here?" Or some dumb thing.

LARRY.   Have you got a match? Yeah.

BURTON.   And I think, This is something I should know about. I'm a writer, I'm supposed to know about these things.

LARRY.   Always a dangerous supposition.

BURTON.   I just shook it off and turned around and leaned against the wall and watched it snow while he went down on me. I came, and he put it away and said thank you, if you believe it, and

44

I said, Have a good life, and went on walking down to the Village. And I never thought about it again. So I'm not completely un-versed in your world.

LARRY. That is gorgeous. With the snow falling. God. I mean it's not *Wuthering Heights*, but ... God.

BURTON. It was very nice, and I never thought about it. And it didn't mean anything, but I've never been sorry it happened or any of that crap.

LARRY. Lord, the innocence and freedom of yesterday.

ANNA. I was just thinking that.

LARRY. Actually, I don't like those ships-that-pass-in-the-night scenes. That doesn't mean that the image of you getting blown in the snow won't haunt me till I die. I think I'll probably be a happier — Did you have your shirt up?

BURTON. I had on a jacket, a scarf, a hat, gloves, galoshes. I had my fly unzipped.

LARRY. You don't care if, in my mind, I sort of push your shirt up to above your navel, and let your pants fall to about mid-thigh, do you?

BURTON. Be my guest. Larry, we're getting ready to go to bed here — I'm just trying to burn a little clock. *(There is a noise outside the door.)*

LARRY. What the hell's that?

ANNA. That's got to be Harrison.

LARRY. Happy New Year, Harrison. You old queen.

ANNA. Oh, he is not.

LARRY. He just doesn't know it. He's going to wake up on his fortieth birthday in a dress.

BURTON. Did he knock?

LARRY. No way, shy as a nun. Has anyone ever really seen a shy nun? *(He opens the door, Pale falls in.)* Oh shit. Scare me to death. Are you hurt?

BURTON. What the hell's happening?

LARRY. It's Pale. Not in the best shape. Are you okay? *(Pale staggers, half on his hands and knees, to the bathroom.)*

ANNA. Absolutely not, Jimmy. No way. I'm sorry. Jimmy! Damnit all! Who the hell does he think he is?

BURTON. Who the hell *is* he?

45

ANNA. Oh, God. He's a maître d' or....

LARRY. Manager.

ANNA. Manager.

LARRY. Of a restaurant.

ANNA. The Il Santalino or something.

LARRY. Da Signate.

ANNA. Over in Short Hills.

LARRY. Montclair.

ANNA. *(Beat.)* New Jersey.

LARRY. If after five attempts, you think you get any points for New Jersey....

BURTON. He just walks in? What the fuck's he doing here? He live in the building?

LARRY. He's Robbie's brother.

BURTON. Oh shit.

LARRY. Yeah, he's pretty crushed.

ANNA. Well, he can be crushed somewhere else. Really. He can't just bulldoze his way in here every time he hangs one on. Is he being sick?

LARRY. I would say affirmative, except I try not to talk like that.

ANNA. Oh, God.

BURTON. It's a little late, gang, for a neighborly visit, you know?

LARRY. *(At the bathroom door.)* Jimmy — are you — yes, he's being sick. Jesus. Doll, are you all right?

PALE. *(Offstage.)* What the fuck do you know, fruit?

LARRY. I beg your pardon?

PALE. *(Offstage.)* What the fuck do you know?

LARRY. What do I know?

PALE. *(Offstage.)* What the fuck do you fuckin' know, fruit?

LARRY. Jimmy, that's one of those questions one never knows whether to answer with hubris or humility. Are you okay?

PALE. *(Offstage.)* Get the fuck out! *(Slams the door in Larry's face.)*

LARRY. In layout design I could whip his ass. I think this would be a good time to relax and finish the champagne.

BURTON. You want him out of here?

46

ANNA. Oh, for godsake. *(Goes to bathroom door.)* Jimmy. Jimmy. Are you — well, obviously he's not all right. Jimmy, what's up? *(Pale opens the door, his face wet, mopping it with a towel, hangs on to her, kisses her.)* Come on. What the hell do you think this is?
BURTON. Hey, fella. What the hell do you think you're doing?
PALE. *(Drops the towel, drops to one knee, holding the wall to steady himself.)* Who the fuck are you?

ANNA. Hey, Burt, come on. Burton, this is Jimmy, Robbie's brother—Jimmy, this is my friend Burton. I feel like an idiot. Larry, shut up. Jimmy, we're not entertaining tonight, so I don't think you can stay.

LARRY. Where the fuck did you come from? What the fuck do you want? It's me, isn't it? You've always wanted to fuck me. You want to have your filthy fuckin' way with me in the hot desert sun . . . Ravage me like I've never been ravaged before.

PALE. You another dancer?
ANNA. Burton's a writer.
PALE. Same thing.
BURTON. Do you need something? Or is this just a friendly visit? Jimmy?
PALE. "Jimmy," shit. Nobody calls me Jimmy. They call me Pale.
BURTON. What?
ANNA. Pale.
BURTON. As in bucket?
ANNA. As in a bucket of brandy. Pale, it's 3 A.M. I know you don't get off work till late, but we're about to call it a ... year here, you know?
BURTON. You need help getting down to the street or something? *(Pale gets up, manages to stumble to a chair, almost turning over a table. Sits.)*
ANNA. Oh, you are in great shape. You look like a bum.
BURTON. What do you mean? He is a bum.
ANNA. He's not a bum.
BURTON. Who the hell is he?
ANNA. I told you, Burton, damnit. He's the maître d' —
LARRY. God! Manager! Of the Da Signate Ristorante in Montclair, New Jersey. Jesus.

47

ANNA.   He has a very demanding job.

BURTON.   Don't we all. You need help, buddy? 'Cause you're not staying.

PALE.   What the fuck do you know?

ANNA.   Very little, I'm sure. About anything.

BURTON.   I know you're leaving. You call tomorrow. Late, okay?

PALE.   About Robbie? Huh? Fuckin' zip.

ANNA.   Pale, it's been two months. More. I'm sorry, but you can't grieve forever. Not even you. *I* can't. He gets drunk, he thinks about him. Guilt and that number.

BURTON.   He's gonna pass out. Unless you intend to put him up here, I'm gonna help him out into the street. I seem to remember we were having a party.

PALE.   You're not "right," are you. You're a little funny.

BURTON.   We'll see if you laugh.

PALE.   *(To Anna.)* Tell your friend good night. Let's go.

BURTON.   You're the one who's leaving, buddy. *(Pale lunges at Burton. Burton, with a deft move, drives Pale straight into a wall head-first. Pale sits on the floor, his back against the wall, staring at them.)*

ANNA.   Burt. Pale. Oh, for godsake.

BURTON.   What the hell does he think he's doing?

ANNA.   *(To a blinking Pale.)* I should have mentioned, Burt teaches akido at the "Y."

BURTON.   Six years, that's the first time I ever used it.

LARRY.   *(Lighting a cigarette.)* Please note, I'm smoking again. Also, that's not the smartest thing to do. He carries a gun.

BURTON.   A what? And you let him in here?

LARRY.   He fell in.

ANNA.   He takes the deposits to the bank at night. I asked; we were right. I don't believe it.

PALE.   What fuckin' accident? No fuckin' accident.

LARRY.   What's that?

PALE.   Robbie and Dominic out in the fuckin' bay — I said there wasn't any fuckin' accident.

ANNA.   Not again, Jimmy — I think we've done that number.

PALE.   What are you wearin' that thing?

LARRY.   What about the accident, Pale?

PALE.   *(To Anna.)* You ain't cold, that thing?

48

ANNA. No. *(To Larry.)* It's nothing, believe me.

BURTON.   Then I'm sorry, fella, we can't serve you here ... after hours, buddy.

PALE.   *(Looks at Burton.)* Who's Bruce Lee? You're cute. You think I can't break a candy ass like him?

ANNA.   When I saw him before, he was saying the mob did it. They have some interest in the restaurant.

LARRY. Oh, please.

BURTON.   When was this you saw him?

LARRY.   There were definitely no mobster types when I went to the restaurant.

PALE.   What assholes. I thought you people was supposed to be *with* it, you're supposed to "swing," you "know what's coming down." Show me a restaurant ain't connected, I'll show you an establishment don't serve food and drink, okay? I can't stay here *(Getting up.)* with you assholes. I got me a reputation to uphold here. You're too stupid for me to stay with.

BURTON.   If you know something —

LARRY.   Or think you do, you should — *(As Burton approaches Pale, Pale decks him; tripping him, kicking him in the groin and again in the back as soon as he hits the floor.)*

ANNA.   Pale — damnit. Burton, are you all right?

PALE.   Nobody does that shit, nobody pulls that shit. *(Burton is up, winded and shocked; they square off, circle.)*

BURTON.   All right, fella, I was being nice; I'm gonna take you apart. I'm gonna enjoy this.

ANNA.   Burton, stop it, goddamnit. Both of you. Come on.

PALE.   Come on, come on — *(He makes a lunge and Burton sends him flying.)*

ANNA.   Burton! Goddamnit, for Christ's sake, this is my apartment! What the fuck do you two think you're doing? *(She steps between them. Burton shoves her aside very roughly; she falls. He clips Pale — Pale sprawls.)* Burton. Goddamnit.

BURTON.   No way, buddy, nobody blind-sides me, no way.

ANNA.   Okay, leave, then, go on. Burton, damnit, I said leave. *(Pushes him away — Pale stands off.)*

BURTON.   I'm not leaving you here with him.

ANNA.   Yes, you are, and now.

BURTON. No way am I leaving you alone with this fucker. *(Pale has sat down.)* Go on, buddy, out.

ANNA. You first, just go — Really, I'm not going to have it. That's not the way I live.

BURTON. We were going to have a party — that son-of-a-bitch comes over; no way.

ANNA. Leave, go on. I'll see you tomorrow. I can't have it.

BURTON. Anna, what kind of a man is going to leave you alone with him? Huh? What's he going to do?

ANNA. Nothing.

BURTON. You don't know him.

ANNA. I know him, he's fine. I can't kick him out, so I'm asking you to leave.

BURTON. I'll kick him out, no problem.

ANNA. Go. Damnit. You're the one I don't know right now.

PALE. You fuckin' him, too? *(A stunned pause.)*

BURTON. What'd you say?

ANNA. Would you please not do this crap?

PALE. Good night.

ANNA. Burton, really, good night.

BURTON. What's he talking about? You're....

ANNA. It's utterly beside the point. Good night. Tomorrow.

BURTON. I'm gonna have to rethink everything here. I mean our whole relationship here. This isn't it. This is nothing I want any part of.

ANNA. Good night. *(Burton gets his coat, goes to the door without looking back, and leaves.)*

PALE. Good night, Bruce.

LARRY. Did you hurt your arm?

ANNA. Oh — no more than I've been hurt every week since I was eight. Pale, you're going to have to — *(Pale puts his arms around her, his hands under her robe.)* Stop it, damnit. I'm not your whore, for you to have every time you get drunk. Stop it. *(Pulls away.)* Goddamnit, both of you with that macho bullshit. Okay, now you. Get it together and get it out of here. Up. Go on.

LARRY. Pale? It's not as butch as Burton, but if you don't leave, I'll hit you over the head with a skillet. I'm not joking.

ANNA.   I should have had you and Burton carry him out. I didn't want them breaking each other's faces out on the street. *Gunfight at the O.K. Corral.*

PALE.   I ain't got it.

LARRY.   You ain't got — don't have what?

PALE.   The gun. I lost the fucker.

ANNA.   When?

PALE.   Last week. It's gone. I ain't got it.

ANNA.   Where? Well, that's a stupid ... Pale, don't stretch out and — Pale? Oh, God....

LARRY.   You don't mean it.

ANNA.   Sleeping like a baby.

LARRY.   Oh, great. He could have broken Burton's back or something — Oh, Lordy. *(He pours them each a glass of champagne.)* Is it too cold to drag him out?

ANNA.   With the anti-freeze he's got in him, he should be good for a month. If he'd had the grace to pass out a minute sooner, Burton'd still be here. I had almost decided if he proposed again I was going to accept him.

LARRY.   That's why you dressed like Lucia di Lammermoor. *(He hands her her glass.)*

ANNA.   Thank you. Happy New Year.

LARRY.   A real auspicious beginning.

ANNA.   I loathe violence. What is that? I could live my life very well, thank you, without ever seeing another straight man.

LARRY.   Me too. Don't hold me to that. What was that about the accident?

ANNA.   Oh, when I saw him last week, he was saying he and his dad and their cronies got to drinking, someone says I saw your fruit brother on the TV with his boyfriend. All the usual fag-baiting braggadocio. Someone ought to off the fucker, embarrassment to the family, that crap. And a couple of nights later, Robbie's dead, so he had no way of knowing if —

LARRY.   Oh, give me a break.

ANNA.   That's what I said. Massive guilt trip.

LARRY.   Good. Serves you right, Pale. I have to carry those fuckin' bags down to my room.

ANNA.   Get them tomorrow.

LARRY.   Never put off till tomorrow what might kill you today. Also, my toothbrush is in there somewhere. God, how it's missed its own glass. Are you going to bed? *(He gets his bags.)*

ANNA.   Yes. Pale? Oh damn.

LARRY.   Get a blanket down from Robbie's room, I guess.

ANNA.   He doesn't like to be covered.

LARRY.   That's right. He'll be sorry. *(Anna turns off the lights. The living room is dark. They are both in their rooms. From off.)* My own bed, my own sheets, my own pillow....

ANNA.   *(From Off.)* Should I set an alarm or something for him, so he doesn't miss work again?

LARRY.   *(From Off.)* They're probably closed tomorrow.

ANNA.   *(From Off.)* Then to hell with it. *(She goes into the bathroom, turns on the light.)* Good night, love.

LARRY.   *(Offstage.)* 'Night, doll. *(Sings.)*
> "At night I wake up with the sheets soaking wet
> There's a freight train runnin'
> Through the middle of my head ...
> And you, you cool my desire.
> Oh ... oh ... oh ... I'm on fire ..."*

(Pale sits up on the sofa. He gets up, looks around, moves to the window, opens it, and steps out onto the fire escape. He walks the distance of the windows, lights a cigarette. Anna comes from the bathroom to her room. After a moment Pale flicks his cigarette out into the night. He comes back into the apartment and walks to her room. The lights fade, music up. Larry is in the kitchen. Coffee has been made, Pale, dressed in one of Anna's robes, comes from her room.)

It does nothing for you. I couldn't wait to sleep the clock around in my own bed. I woke up at eight.

PALE.   *(Sleepy.)* What time is it?

LARRY.   About nine. You off today?

PALE.   Yeah.

LARRY.   Sleep late, for godsake; once, anyway.

PALE.   Can't do it.

LARRY.   I made coffee, you don't use it. What about tea?

PALE.   Whatta you got?

LARRY.   *(Looking through cabinet.)* We got: English Breakfast, Irish

*See Special Note on Music on copyright page.

Breakfast, something that tastes exactly like I imagine burned rubber tires would taste....

PALE.   Lapsang Souchong.

LARRY.   You want it, you'd be doing us a favor.

PALE.   You got no plain orange pekoe tea?

LARRY.   — Jasmine, Sleepytime, Red Zinger, camomile. And plain Red Rose orange pekoe tea. *(Puts the bag in a mug.)* The water's still hot. I thought your familiarity with the finer foods of life —

PALE.   Stop. Whattaya doin'? You gonna make a pot o' tea, you gonna make one cup? It's not even economical.

LARRY.   We actually have a teapot, but I've never seen it used for anything except to put flowers in. *(Takes it out of cabinet.)*

PALE.   Get out, go on, you're useless. I thought you clowns were supposed to be worthwhile in the kitchen at least.

LARRY.   I never really claimed any expertise in the area. You cook?

PALE.   *(Turns up heat under water until it boils.)* I'd better cook. Cook ain't in, I'm it. What? Six — eight times cook don't show, snowstorm, somethin', I gotta cook. I'm okay. *(Pours water in pot, empties it.)*

LARRY.   There? Professionally? I've been to your place; twice, actually. It's very good.

PALE.   Yeah, I told the cook people couldn't tell the difference. He didn't like it. Next time it snowed he slept inna kitchen. *Gourmet* magazine, they print recipes from like these famous restaurants; I take in the magazine, twice now. I say, So how come you left out the paprika in one; in the other, how come there ain't no lemon juice and no nutmeg? And the butter ain't clarified? He says, Okay, they'll make it at home, then they'll come here and think, Son-of-a-bitch, that man's just a better cook than I am. *(He puts the water and three tea bags in the pot, looks for a tea towel, covers the pot with it.)*

LARRY.   Whatever you're doing, I'm impressed.

PALE.   What? Twenty years the restaurant business, I can't make a pot of tea, I'm in trouble.

LARRY.   You know, it's very unlikely anyone did your family the favor of arranging Robbie's accident.

53

PALE. I don't wanta talk about it, okay?

LARRY. This would be the situation where the little boy says, "I hate Daddy and I want him to die," and two days later Daddy goes off to the hospital and doesn't come home again. And the little boy thinks it's his fault.

PALE. Yeah? That mighta been the night the angels decided to listen to the little boy.

LARRY. I don't think so.

PALE. That's the way Catholics think; we're fucked.

LARRY. It all sounds very unlikely.

PALE. Yeah, one side of my brain knows that — the other side drinks.

LARRY. Anna said she might be wrong, but she doesn't remember your wife at Robbie's funeral.

PALE. She wasn't there.

LARRY. So she's still in Coral Gables?

PALE. You remember everything everybody says, huh?

LARRY. It's a gift.

PALE. She couldn't take the heat, so she took the kids. Who the fuck cares? I'm home three hours a night, work seventeen hours some days; more'n sixty-five hours a week. I get off midnight, I gotta unwind; I get home at two, I'm up at five. Who can live with that?

LARRY. How can you?

PALE. I'm used to it.

LARRY. You'll burn yourself out, too. She should have taken a job as a waitress at the restaurant.

PALE. You got a real sense of humor there, that could be valuable to you. Her work? Not while I'm makin' nine hundred bucks a week. Six of it off the books, more like nineteen hundred.

LARRY. Jesus.

PALE. I bust my butt, don't worry.

LARRY. So you're divorced?

PALE. What's with questions, this hour the morning? I might want to experience the day here. Take inventory, somethin'. Her give me a divorce? She split, you should see how religious she got. The medals, the saints, the candles, never seen such crap. I coulda dragged her ass back. Who needs it? Sicka lookin' at her. Married

54

a week outta school — what'd I know, I'm eighteen. It was good about six days. *(Pouring tea, adds milk.)*

LARRY. Milk?

PALE. Yeah, it — like — ties up the tannic acid, it don't burn your guts.

LARRY. There's lemon in the fridge.

PALE. Lemon'll kill ya.

LARRY. Citric acid's vitamin C — cure anything.

PALE. Acid's acid. *(Phone rings; we hear Larry's voice.)*

LARRY'S VOICE. Hello. Neither Anna nor I can come to the phone just now. Please leave a message when you hear the beep. *(Pause — beep.)*

BURTON'S VOICE. Uh, Anna? It's Burton. Listen, I think I had too much blow last night, I —

PALE. He hang up? *(Pause.)* He hang up?

LARRY. She picked it up in the bedroom.

PALE. *(Into phone.)* You got somethin' talk about, Bruce, come over, we'll talk. *(Laughs.)* He hung up.

LARRY. *(Lighting a cigarette.)* You are hazardous to people's health, Pale.

ANNA. *(Enters, in jeans and T-shirt.)* Goddamnit, Pale, what the hell do you think you're doing? That phone call happened to be — oh, real cute. Thanks. *(She slams down on the sofa. He goes to her. Sips his tea, offers her some.)* That looks strong.

PALE. You want a cup?

ANNA. I guess.

PALE. You want some eggs? *(He pours her a cup of tea.)*

LARRY. He cooks.

ANNA. No, I don't want to admit I'm still awake. Uh, Pale....

LARRY. I'm going to take a shower.

ANNA. In a minute, okay? Pale, would you do me a favor?

PALE. Sure.

ANNA. I don't want you to think that we've started something here.

PALE. ... How come?

ANNA. I just don't. We're apples and oranges.

PALE. Yeah? Who's the apple and who's the orange?

ANNA. Pale.

PALE.   You ever had that apple tart, glazed with marmalade?

ANNA.   No, I haven't. I have to work; you have work to do.

PALE.   Yeah? You get the job?

ANNA.   What? Yes. I'm making a dance for a very important concert and it has me a little hysterical and it's occupying my time completely. This just isn't for me. I'm sorry if I led you on in any way. I don't feel well, and I'm not up for one of your scenes, but I'd like to not see you anymore.

PALE.   How come?

ANNA.   I don't know. I think you're dangerous.

PALE.   Bullshit. You walk down the street, a brick falls on your head.

ANNA.   But not in my apartment.

PALE.   You gonna never leave your room, what?

ANNA.   I might.

PALE.   How come you don't feel good?

ANNA.   I'm tired, my stomach's upset.

PALE.   Who wouldn't be tired after what we did — ?

ANNA.   Pale.

PALE.   I'm tired, too; I'm fuckin' hung out to dry here. That tea's no good for a bad stomach. You want some milk?

ANNA.   No. Please, Pale.

PALE.   You're a real different person in the sack than you are standin' up.

ANNA.   I know.

PALE.   Which one's the lie? Were you fakin' it?

ANNA.   I'm not lying now. And no, it isn't possible for me to fake it in bed.

PALE.   You kiddin' me? Easiest thing in the world. Done it all my life. Half the time I'd fake it, too fuckin' tired to have interest. My ol' lady'd run in and douche herself, come back feelin' fucked, cuddle up to me; I didn't know whether to hate the bitch for believin' me or for flushin' me out. Both of 'em lies. Lies happen like every ten seconds. Half the people you see on the street don't mean a thing they're doin'. Hug up some bitch, don't mean nothin' to them. Bitch smilin' up into his eyes, have more fun pushin' the bastard through a sausage grinder. My brother

Sammy, older'n me, kissed his bride, said he wanted to bite the lips off her. People ain't easy.

ANNA.   I know.

PALE.   You said last night in the sack you ain't been with nobody since a month ago when you was with me. I ain't either. I figger one more time, we got us a hat trick. I got a vacation comin' up. I thought we'd go someplace.

ANNA.   I'm working.

PALE.   Hawaii, Brazil. See places.

ANNA.   Really, Pale. Really.

LARRY.   *(After a long pause.)* I think I should go straighten my room.

PALE.   Naw, you stay here, like she wanted. I'll split. I don't hurt people. *(He goes into her room.)*

ANNA.   No cracks, okay.

LARRY.   Okay.

ANNA.   No jokes.

LARRY.   Even if it kills me.

ANNA.   May I go to your room and lock the door? I don't want to see him.

LARRY.   Of course you may.

PALE.   *(He has put his pants on, but nothing else; comes from her room.)* No, I don't like it. You're gettin' me mad here. Lived with that bitch sixteen years, all we ever do is yell, never touched her once. Never felt nothin' for her.

ANNA.   How would you be with someone you felt something for?

PALE.   I never felt nothin' for nobody. How do I know? Whatta you want, a contract here? I'll write it out: I ever hit you, take my car or somethin'. What's causin' this crap?

ANNA.   Pale, I don't even know how this nonsense started; it never should have.

PALE.   It did.

ANNA.   It didn't. Well, it did and it shouldn't have. I'm tired and sick, and I've got work to do.

PALE.   Everybody's off today.

ANNA.   Then I've got to sleep; you don't sleep, I sleep.

PALE. So we'll sleep.

ANNA. No ... definitely not; I'm tired.

PALE. Me too. So what? My pants look like a pig's wearin' 'em, I got a hangover here, I'm puttin' on weight, I'm losin' my hair, and you're talkin' like that? I'm not dangerous. You don't think I'm dangerous; you think you're afraid of me is what you think.

ANNA. Okay, fine.

PALE. Why? *(Pause.)* You're afraid you might get interested. Have to feel somethin'.

ANNA. I feel, Pale, all the time. I'm a crackerjack feeler, thank you. *(Pause. To Larry.)* I'll go to your room.

LARRY. Sure. If he breaks the door in, somebody else pays for it.

PALE. I don't break in doors.

LARRY. I did once. Nearly killed myself. Cost three hundred dollars to replace.

PALE. Annie! Hey!

ANNA. *(At Larry's door.)* Pale, don't do this.

PALE. Do what? What am I doin'? You're the one doin' here.

ANNA. Oh, God. I'll try to say this so you can understand where ... my point of view. I almost said "where I'm coming from." I have a friend that I'm seeing, Pale, and —

PALE. Who's that, Bruce?

ANNA. Burton. And we see —

PALE. You like him so much, why ain't you makin' it with him?

ANNA. ... and we see things very similarly, and share a great deal, and I like being with him. I, at least, would like to give us the time to see if we're as compatible as we seem to be.

PALE. No, I can tell you.

ANNA. And I'm at a time in my life when — well, I just don't feel like fucking around. Sleeping around.

PALE. So don't.

ANNA. Pale, I have never had a personal life. I wasn't scared of it, I just had no place for it, it wasn't important. And all that is different now and I'm very vulnerable, I'm not going to be prey to something I don't want. I'm too easy. Go somewhere else.

PALE. I come to you.

ANNA. No. I said no. I don't want this. I'm not strong enough to kick you out physically. Why are you being so damned truculent? I said I don't like you. I don't want to know you. I don't want to see you again. There is no reason for you to come here. I have nothing for you. I don't like you and I'm frightened of you. *(Pale looks at her, goes into the bedroom, comes out with his clothes. Goes to his cup of tea, finishing it. He doesn't look at her; they both stare at him.)*

PALE. *(Not looking up from tying his shoes.)* What does that mean, "truculent"?

LARRY. Fierce, or actually, think, uh, "like a truck."

PALE. *(Mumbles.)* Like a truck. Great. *(He finishes and goes to her, kisses her and leaves. Anna is on the brink of tears to the end of the scene.)*

LARRY. I didn't think you'd get rid of him by telling him to go. You say, "I'm desperately in love with you, never leave my side; I want to have your baby," and they'll leave.

ANNA. Could you go see if he actually is leaving?

LARRY. He actually is leaving.

ANNA. Go watch, I'm not kidding. Jesus, I reek of Jimmy.

LARRY. A little brandy-perspiration and cologne. Not that bad, really. As he said, he's clean.

ANNA. The whole bedroom reeks of him. God. I'm going to have a shower, make the bed with clean sheets, and sleep the entire day. *(Leaving.)* Thanks for staying for that. *(She is gone.)*

LARRY. *(Half calling to her.)* Think nothing of it. It was a completely new experience for me. And that is something I've never enjoyed. I'm not really that improvisational. I like having a rough copy to work from, at least. Something to go by. *(She reenters with an enormous wad of sheets.)*

ANNA. What?

LARRY. Nothing.

ANNA. I'm sick of the age I'm living in. I don't like feeling ripped off and scared.

LARRY. *(Not campy.)* You'd rather be pillaged and raped?

ANNA. I'm *being* pillaged and raped. I'm being pillaged and I'm being raped. And I don't like it. *(Stands in the middle of the pile of sheets. All the wind goes out of her.)*

LARRY. What? What is it, doll? Huh? *(Anna almost cries; her shoulders shake.)*

ANNA. Ohhhhh! *I feel miserable!* Oh damnit all. Did he leave?

LARRY. Yes.

ANNA. Aw, Jesus. Is he still out there, or did you see him drive off?

LARRY. I saw him drive off. If you didn't want him to go, you sure fooled me. It's okay, doll.

ANNA. It's not okay, doll; it fucking sucks.

LARRY. Okay, it sucks. You're absolutely right, it fucking sucks. Man, does it suck. It sucks so bad. God, does it suck.

ANNA. Don't. Come on.

LARRY. What?

ANNA. Goddamnit, I can't take it. *(She goes to the closet, gets her coat.)* I'm gonna have to see some more kids tomorrow — I'm working with four, I think I need six. Three couples. If I can't have a life at least I can work.

LARRY. Where you going?

ANNA. To Fred's studio. No one will be there today; I can get something done.

LARRY. Work here.

ANNA. No, no offense, but I want to be by myself.

LARRY. I'll leave.

ANNA. No.

LARRY. Eat something first.

ANNA. No, I'm not hungry. I'll pick up something later. Happy New Year. Get some rest.

LARRY. Well, don't just whip out of here, take a shower first. *(She is at the door, coat on, bag in her hand, looking for her keys. She looks up at him steadily for a moment, studio keys in her hand. The music rises. She exits, closing the door behind her. Blackout. Burton stands C., still, rather in a daze. He holds a script. Larry comes from his room putting on a sweatshirt. The door remains open; it's a gray day.)*

Sorry — I had but nothing on. Foul day, huh? *(Beat.)* You want to get the door? *(Pause.)* Burt? You want to get the door? *(Pause. He goes to shut the door.)*

BURTON. Is Anna here?

LARRY. No. She's been busting her butt, you know, on the piece. It's glorious, of course.

BURTON. I'm, uh, I want to see it.

LARRY. It starts tonight, so she's probably there. It's only on the four nights — which is a long run for that kind of thing, if you can believe it. It's wonderful. I saw a tech run-through last night — It's miles and away the best piece on the program.

BURTON. She hasn't answered any of my messages. I wrote; I've been calling for a month.

LARRY. Maybe our machine isn't working; I don't think we're getting our messages....

BURTON. No, that's okay, you don't have to do that.

LARRY. ... Good. You been working?

BURTON. Yeah, I did ... the city thing. Most of it. I wanted to — I wanted her to read it.

LARRY. That's great. She'd love to. So would I.

BURTON. No, I don't think I'm ready for ... well, okay. You're in it, sure. Don't pass it around.

LARRY. I'm in it?

BURTON. Nobody's safe around a writer. I thought you knew that.

LARRY. What do I do? Never mind, I'll find out. You want a drink?

BURTON. No, I haven't been drinking. Sure, what you got?

LARRY. Anything. Well, actually, vodka and Wild Turkey.

BURTON. Wild Turkey neat.

LARRY. Why not?

BURTON. Has she been seeing him?

LARRY. "Him"?

BURTON. Yeah.

LARRY. *(Making two drinks, vodka on the rocks.)* I'm wondering what my procedure is here. We haven't talked about anything. She's not been out one night this month. But it kinda doesn't matter. I mean, except work. She comes home, I say, Hi, how was it, and she says, It's going well but it's difficult, and I say, You want something to eat, and she says, I stopped by some Chinese place on the way home, and she makes a drink and picks up a book and I go out to eat, and when I come home she's in her room

61

with the light on and the door closed. Reading, I presume. She's working. But I *can* testify that the work she's doing is phenomenal. It's great.

BURTON.   Then she's not seeing him?

LARRY.   Burton, at least say, Good, she's working, or, Terrific, the work's good. Nothing else is important. She's already got a commission from it; no one's even seen it except a few big-wigs.

BURTON.   *(Drinking, second sip.)* What the hell is this?

LARRY.   What?

BURTON.   I asked for Turkey up; this is vodka rocks.

LARRY.   I'm sorry.

BURTON.   That's okay.

LARRY.   No, that's just my mind. *(Pours Burton's drink into his, makes another.)*

BURTON.   So, has she been seeing him?

LARRY.   I thought I answered that.

BURTON.   What'd you say?

LARRY.   ... What'd I say? You tell me.

BURTON.   *(Thinking.)* You said — I was listening; I was just listening too closely. You said, "I'm wondering about my procedure. We haven't talked at all; she's not been out one night in a month, but it kinda doesn't matter, she comes home, I say, Hi — "

LARRY.   Stop. That's phenomenal.

BURTON.   What? She's not been out one night this month?

LARRY.   I said it kinda doesn't matter.

BURTON.   What does that mean?

LARRY.   It doesn't matter if she's seen him. It doesn't matter. The dance she's done is Pale and Anna. No, he hasn't been over. No, she hasn't seen him; it doesn't matter.

BURTON.   Is that what it's called? Pale and Anna? Pale and me? What music are they using?

LARRY.   You're not thinking. You've seen Fred's stuff; when have you ever heard music? It's a synthesized kind of city noise, with a foghorn and gulls and — it's here. This loft. Only more so. It's kind of epic. Well, for twelve minutes.

BURTON.   How do you know it's supposed to be he?

LARRY.   Well, for one thing, I've never seen a man on stage in a dance — it's a man and a — It's very startling. It just has to do with the center of gravity, I guess, but ... or something. I mean it's a regular man — dancing like a man dances — in a bar or something, with his girl. You've never seen anything like it. I can't describe a dance; you might as well try to describe a piece of music.

BURTON.   No, I know what you mean. I have this problem I'm trying to cope with here. I was a rich kid, you know.

LARRY.   I know.

BURTON.   And I've never really — I've always had pretty much my own — I've never lost anything before. Or, I've never lost. Before. *(Pause.)* See, what gets to me is, I keep feeling angry. You know, I could tear the shithead apart.

LARRY.   I know.

BURTON.   I could. But, you know, that doesn't mean anything. What's bothering me is, I keep feeling "Fuck *her,*" you know? — and then I know that that's not really what I'm feeling — that's just a protective mechanism sort of thing that I've always used so I wouldn't lose. You know? 'Cause I've never lost. And I don't really feel "Fuck her" at all. That's just my immune system defending me.

LARRY.   It's a handy thing to have.

BURTON.   *(Setting his glass on the table.)* Hit me.

LARRY.   I beg your pardon? Oh, another, sure. *(Pours, leaves the bottle.)* It's perfectly natural you'd be pissed.

BURTON.   Well see ... uh ... I think you were supposed to say, "Hell, the race isn't over yet, kid, hang in there and fight."

LARRY.   I'm sorry, Burton. "Win one for the Gipper" sticks in my craw.

BURTON.   That's all right. So, I guess she really is in love with someone. We ought to celebrate. How's he feel about her?

LARRY.   His entire mechanism is beyond my pale, doll. Anyway, we've not seen him. He hasn't come around. I would say he feels pretty much the same, but she threw him out so....

BURTON.   She what? She threw him out? Boy, she is a piece of work, isn't she? And then goes off and makes a dance about him, great.

LARRY.   She's had a very protected life. I mean, she's never had to even carry her own passport or plane tickets — she's not had to make her own way much.

BURTON. Yeah, I know. So what's she planning to do with her life? Live here with you?

LARRY. *(Pause.)* I ... uh ... think I'll duck that one, if you don't mind.

BURTON. Sorry, I didn't intend that to sound like it did.

LARRY. No, actually that's very vivid. Put like that. *(Makes himself another drink.)* And by extension, what the fuck am I doing?

BURTON. Well, listen, it's none of my business. Tell her, you know, what we said, if you want to. Or not.

LARRY. *(Beat.)* Huh?... Oh, uh ... no, I definitely will.

BURTON. This isn't the way I was hoping....

LARRY. Tell me about it.

BURTON. Well ... I got work. Read that, let me know what you think. I don't know. Give it to her. Tell her I'd like to hear — you know — what she thought about its — whatever.

LARRY. It's starting to snow, Burton, it's getting dark. Surely we could find a welcoming doorway somewhere on the block.

BURTON. *(Smiles.)* Are you going to make me sorry I told you that?

LARRY. No. Thought I should mention it.

BURTON. I just haven't felt that open to the world since those days. Have a good life. *(He leaves. Larry stands in the middle of the room. Music up, lights fade. The apartment is dark; it is after midnight. Anna unlocks the door and comes in. She is in a party dress and a coat. She goes immediately toward the back without turning on the light, taking off her coat.)*

PALE. I'm here. Don't be scared.

ANNA. Oh, God!

PALE. Don't be scared. I'm stone-cold sober.

ANNA. I'm half drunk. How the hell'd you get in?

PALE. Your friend gave me a key.

ANNA. Larry? Why?

PALE. He come by the bar, he left me a note and the key and shit. The ticket.

ANNA. What ticket?

PALE. I saw your dance tonight. *(Pause.)* I looked for you, I didn't see you.

ANNA. I was hiding in the light booth.

PALE.   You shoulda had Robbie for it. That guy didn't look right. He moved okay, he dances good, but he didn't look right.

ANNA.   ... I did it for Robbie, actually. In my mind Robbie did it.

PALE.   I could tell. *(Pause.)* It wasn't what I thought it'd be.

ANNA.   ... Me either.

PALE.   The other stuff — those first two things was shit. That's why I never went to no modern dance. I knew that's what it was gonna be. I almost had to leave. I didn't stay for that piece after yours.

ANNA.   You would have hated it.

PALE.   Your thing was good.

ANNA.   Thank you.

PALE.   *(Pause.)* It was real good. Everybody stood up and yelled.

ANNA.   Eight or ten people stood up.

PALE.   How'd that feel when they did that?

ANNA.   I was very surprised. I was afraid everyone would hate it. It was a relief.

PALE.   Made me feel good, too. *(Pause.)* That was me and you up there. Only we ain't never danced. I could probably sue you for that.

ANNA.   Probably.

PALE.   I was kind — it's kinda embarrassing ... to see somebody being you up there.

ANNA.   Yes, it is.

PALE.   He did okay. He moves good. She was good. She ain't as pretty as you.

ANNA.   What are you doing going to a dance in the middle of the — Did you take off work?

PALE.   Shit. Yeah, I quit. Bust my nuts twenty years, that guy. Been managing three years, not one day off. I'm tending bar at Danny's. You know ... Ray? Fuckin' vacation. Work eight hours, like not workin'. *(Pause.)* You didn't go to the party? I thought there was a party for you.

ANNA.   ... I went; it was too noisy. Larry said he'd be here. I came home.

PALE.   You been set up. Me too. He said he'd be here. *(A long pause.)*

ANNA.   Pale ... I don't want this. *(She begins to cry softly.)*

PALE. I know. I don't want it, too.

ANNA. What'd he say? The bastard. In the note?

PALE. I read it ten times already. I wasn't gonna come. I almost know it by heart. *(Fishes it out of his pocket, hands it to her.)*

ANNA. *(Trying to read it, gives up.)* That's okay. I can't....

PALE. ... What?

ANNA. I can't read it.

PALE. ... You cryin'? Somebody's always cryin' at your house.

ANNA. I know. I'm sorry. *(Hands it back to him.)* I can't read it.

PALE. It says: "Pale, doll. Here's a ticket for the program tonight and my keys. We're going to the cast party and won't be home until three. I don't know how you're doing, but Anna is in pretty bad shape. This isn't opera, this is life, why should love always be tragic? Burn this." *(He hands it to her. She folds it into a tent, puts it in an ashtray.)* I been in pretty bad shape here, too. I'm thirty-six years old, I got a wife, I got two kids, I never felt nothin' like this.

ANNA. ... I ... uh ... I haven't either.

PALE. I don't know what to do with myself here.

ANNA. I know. *(She lights a match, puts it under Larry's note; they watch it burn.)*

PALE. I thought you didn't like me, so I got lost. You know? 'Cause I didn't want you to do something you didn't like.

ANNA. I know. I was having a pretty difficult time not calling you.

PALE. I didn't know. *(Pause.)* I'm real scared here.

ANNA. I don't want this.... Oh, Lord, I didn't want this....

PALE. I know. I don't want it, either. *(He stands beside one end of the sofa; she sits at the other. They look at each other.)* I didn't expect nothin' like this. *(He reaches his hand toward her; she reaches toward him. They touch. He moves over the back of the sofa and sits at the other end. She lies down, her back against his chest.)* I'm gonna cry all over your hair. *(Curtain.)*

PROPERTY LIST

Cigarette (lit) (ANNA)
Drink (ANNA)
Groceries (LARRY)
Bottle of vodka (ANNA, LARRY)
Juice (BURTON)
Wristwatch (BURTON)
Coffee (ANNA)
Bottle of brandy (PALE)
Glass for brandy (PALE)
Wristwatch (PALE)
Afghan (PALE)
Coffee cup (ANNA)
Pistol (LARRY)
Wallet (PALE)
Script (ANNA, BURTON)
Bottle of champagne (ANNA)
Flute glasses (ANNA)
3 huge suitcases (LARRY)
Pack of cigarettes (LARRY)
Lighter or matches (LARRY, PALE)
Cigarette (PALE)
Teabags (LARRY, PALE)
Mug (LARRY)
Teapot (LARRY)
Boiled water (LARRY)
Tea towel (PALE)
Milk (PALE)
Tea cup (PALE)
Sheets (ANNA)
Bag (ANNA)
Studio keys (ANNA)
Drinking glasses (LARRY)
Ice cubes (LARRY)
Bottle of Wild Turkey (LARRY)
Note (PALE)
Ashtray (ANNA)
Matches (ANNA)

SOUND EFFECTS

Intercom buzzer
Radiator noise (heat)
Phone ring
Distant bell

NEW PLAYS

★ **THE CREDEAUX CANVAS by Keith Bunin.** A forged painting leads to tragedy among friends. "There is that moment between adolescence and middle age when being disaffected looks attractive. Witness the enduring appeal of Prince Hamlet, Jake Barnes and James Dean, on the stage, page and screen. Or, more immediately, take a look at the lithe young things in THE CREDEAUX CANVAS..." *–NY Times.* "THE CREDEAUX CANVAS is the third recent play about painters...it turned out to be the best of the lot, better even than most plays about non-painters." *–NY Magazine.* [2M, 2W] ISBN: 0-8222-1838-0

★ **THE DIARY OF ANNE FRANK by Frances Goodrich and Albert Hackett, newly adapted by Wendy Kesselman.** A transcendently powerful new adaptation in which Anne Frank emerges from history a living, lyrical, intensely gifted young girl. "Undeniably moving. It shatters the heart. The evening never lets us forget the inhuman darkness waiting to claim its incandescently human heroine." *–NY Times.* "A sensitive, stirring and thoroughly engaging new adaptation." *–NY Newsday.* "A powerful new version that moves the audience to gasps, then tears." *–A.P.* "One of the year's ten best." *– Time Magazine.* [5M, 5W, 3 extras] ISBN: 0-8222-1718-X

★ **THE BOOK OF LIZ by David Sedaris and Amy Sedaris.** Sister Elizabeth Donderstock makes the cheese balls that support her religious community, but feeling unappreciated among the Squeamish, she decides to try her luck in the outside world. "...[a] delightfully off-key, off-color hymn to clichés we all live by, whether we know it or not." *–NY Times.* "Good-natured, goofy and frequently hilarious..." *–NY Newsday.* "...[THE BOOK OF LIZ] may well be the world's first Amish picaresque...hilarious..." *–Village Voice.* [2M, 2W (doubling, flexible casting to 8M, 7W)] ISBN: 0-8222-1827-5

★ **JAR THE FLOOR by Cheryl L. West.** A quartet of black women spanning four generations makes up this hilarious and heartwarming dramatic comedy. "...a moving and hilarious account of a black family sparring in a Chicago suburb..." *–NY Magazine.* "...heart-to-heart confrontations and surprising revelations...first-rate..." *–NY Daily News.* "...unpretentious good feelings...bubble through West's loving and humorous play...." *–Star-Ledger.* "...one of the wisest plays I've seen in ages...[from] a master playwright." *–USA Today.* [5W] ISBN: 0-8222-1809-7

★ **THIEF RIVER by Lee Blessing.** Love between two men over decades is explored in this incisive portrait of coming to terms with who you are. "Mr. Blessing unspools the plot ingeniously, skipping back and forth in time as the details require...an absorbing evening." *–NY Times.* "...wistful and sweet-spirited..." *–Variety.* [6M] ISBN: 0-8222-1839-9

★ **THE BEGINNING OF AUGUST by Tom Donaghy.** When Jackie's wife abruptly and mysteriously leaves him and their infant daughter, a pungently comic reevaluation of suburban life ensues. "Donaghy holds a cracked mirror up to the contemporary American family, anatomizing its frailties and miscommunications in fractured language that can be both funny and poignant." *–The Philadelphia Inquirer.* "...[A] sharp, eccentric new comedy. Pungently funny...fresh and precise..." *–LA Times.* [3M, 2W] ISBN: 0-8222-1786-4

★ **OUTSTANDING MEN'S MONOLOGUES 2001–2002 and OUTSTANDING WOMEN'S MONOLOGUES 2001–2002 edited by Craig Pospisil.** Drawn exclusively from Dramatists Play Service publications, these collections for actors feature over fifty monologues each and include an enormous range of voices, subject matter and characters. MEN'S ISBN: 0-8222-1821-6 WOMEN'S ISBN: 0-8222-1822-4

DRAMATISTS PLAY SERVICE, INC.
440 Park Avenue South, New York, NY 10016 212-683-8960 Fax 212-213-1539
postmaster@dramatists.com www.dramatists.com

NEW PLAYS

★ **A LESSON BEFORE DYING by Romulus Linney, based on the novel by Ernest J. Gaines.** An innocent young man is condemned to death in backwoods Louisiana and must learn to die with dignity. "The story's wrenching power lies not in its outrage but in the almost inexplicable grace the characters must muster as their only resistance to being treated like lesser beings." *–The New Yorker.* "Irresistable momentum and a cathartic explosion...a powerful inevitability." *–NY Times.* [5M, 2W] ISBN: 0-8222-1785-6

★ **BOOM TOWN by Jeff Daniels.** A searing drama mixing small-town love, politics and the consequences of betrayal. "...a brutally honest, contemporary foray into classic themes, exploring what moves people to lie, cheat, love and dream. By BOOM TOWN's climactic end there are no secrets, only bare truth." *–Oakland Press.* "...some of the most electrifying writing Daniels has ever done..." *–Ann Arbor News.* [2M, 1W] ISBN: 0-8222-1760-0

★ **INCORRUPTIBLE by Michael Hollinger.** When a motley order of medieval monks learns their patron saint no longer works miracles, a larcenous, one-eyed minstrel shows them an outrageous new way to pay old debts. "A lightning-fast farce, rich in both verbal and physical humor." *–American Theatre.* "Everything fits snugly in this funny, endearing black comedy...an artful blend of the mock-formal and the anachronistically breezy...A piece of remarkably dexterous craftsmanship." *–Philadelphia Inquirer.* "A farcical romp, scintillating and irreverent." *–Philadelphia Weekly.* [5M, 3W] ISBN: 0-8222-1787-2

★ **CELLINI by John Patrick Shanley.** Chronicles the life of the original "Renaissance Man," Benvenuto Cellini, the sixteenth-century Italian sculptor and man-about-town. Adapted from the autobiography of Benvenuto Cellini, translated by J. Addington Symonds. "[Shanley] has created a convincing Cellini, not neglecting his dark side, and a trim, vigorous, fast-moving show." *–BackStage.* "Very entertaining...With brave purpose, the narrative undermines chronology before untangling it...touching and funny..." *–NY Times.* [7M, 2W (doubling)] ISBN: 0-8222-1808-9

★ **PRAYING FOR RAIN by Robert Vaughan.** Examines a burst of fatal violence and its aftermath in a suburban high school. "Thought provoking and compelling." *–Denver Post.* "Vaughan's powerful drama offers hope and possibilities." *–Theatre.com.* "[The play] doesn't put forth compact, tidy answers to the problem of youth violence. What it does offer is a compelling exploration of the forces that influence an individual's choices, and of the proverbial lifelines—be they familial, communal, religious or political—that tragically slacken when society gives in to apathy, fear and self-doubt..." *–Westword.* "...a symphony of anger..." *–Gazette Telegraph.* [4M, 3W] ISBN: 0-8222-1807-0

★ **GOD'S MAN IN TEXAS by David Rambo.** When a young pastor takes over one of the most prestigious Baptist churches from a rip-roaring old preacher-entrepreneur, all hell breaks loose. "...the pick of the litter of all the works at the Humana Festival..." *–Providence Journal.* "...a wealth of both drama and comedy in the struggle for power..." *–LA Times.* "...the first act is so funny...deepens in the second act into a sobering portrait of fear, hope and self-delusion..." *–Columbus Dispatch.* [3M] ISBN: 0-8222-1801-1

★ **JESUS HOPPED THE 'A' TRAIN by Stephen Adly Guirgis.** A probing, intense portrait of lives behind bars at Rikers Island. "...fire-breathing...whenever it appears that JESUS is settling into familiar territory, it slides right beneath expectations into another, fresher direction. It has the courage of its intellectual restlessness...[JESUS HOPPED THE 'A' TRAIN] has been written in flame." *–NY Times.* [4M, 1W] ISBN: 0-8222-1799-6

DRAMATISTS PLAY SERVICE, INC.
440 Park Avenue South, New York, NY 10016 212-683-8960 Fax 212-213-1539
postmaster@dramatists.com www.dramatists.com

NEW PLAYS

★ **THE CIDER HOUSE RULES, PARTS 1 & 2 by Peter Parnell, adapted from the novel by John Irving.** Spanning eight decades of American life, this adaptation from the Irving novel tells the story of Dr. Wilbur Larch, founder of the St. Cloud's, Maine orphanage and hospital, and of the complex father-son relationship he develops with the young orphan Homer Wells. "...luxurious digressions, confident pacing...an enterprise of scope and vigor..." *—NY Times.* "...The fact that I can't wait to see Part 2 only begins to suggest just how good it is..." *—NY Daily News.* "...engrossing...an odyssey that has only one major shortcoming: It comes to an end." *—Seattle Times.* "...outstanding...captures the humor, the humility...of Irving's 588-page novel..." *—Seattle Post-Intelligencer.* [9M, 10W, doubling, flexible casting] PART 1 ISBN: 0-8222-1725-2 PART 2 ISBN: 0-8222-1726-0

★ **TEN UNKNOWNS by Jon Robin Baitz.** An iconoclastic American painter in his seventies has his life turned upside down by an art dealer and his ex-boyfriend. "...breadth and complexity...a sweet and delicate harmony rises from the four cast members...Mr. Baitz is without peer among his contemporaries in creating dialogue that spontaneously conveys a character's social context and moral limitations..." *—NY Times.* "...darkly funny, brilliantly desperate comedy...TEN UNKNOWNS vibrates with vital voices." *—NY Post.* [3M, 1W] ISBN: 0-8222-1826-7

★ **BOOK OF DAYS by Lanford Wilson.** A small-town actress playing St. Joan struggles to expose a murder. "...[Wilson's] best work since *Fifth of July*...An intriguing, prismatic and thoroughly engrossing depiction of contemporary small-town life with a murder mystery at its core...a splendid evening of theater..." *—Variety.* "...fascinating...a densely populated, unpredictable little world." *—St. Louis Post-Dispatch.* [6M, 5W] ISBN: 0-8222-1767-8

★ **THE SYRINGA TREE by Pamela Gien.** Winner of the 2001 Obie Award. A breathtakingly beautiful tale of growing up white in apartheid South Africa. "Instantly engaging, exotic, complex, deeply shocking...a thoroughly persuasive transport to a time and a place...stun[s] with the power of a gut punch..." *—NY Times.* "Astonishing...affecting ...[with] a dramatic and heartbreaking conclusion...A deceptive sweet simplicity haunts THE SYRINGA TREE..." *—A.P.* [1W (or flexible cast)] ISBN: 0-8222-1792-9

★ **COYOTE ON A FENCE by Bruce Graham.** An emotionally riveting look at capital punishment. "The language is as precise as it is profane, provoking both troubling thought and the occasional cheerful laugh...will change you a little before it lets go of you." *—Cincinnati CityBeat.* "...excellent theater in every way..." *—Philadelphia City Paper.* [3M, 1W] ISBN: 0-8222-1738-4

★ **THE PLAY ABOUT THE BABY by Edward Albee.** Concerns a young couple who have just had a baby and the strange turn of events that transpire when they are visited by an older man and woman. "An invaluable self-portrait of sorts from one of the few genuinely great living American dramatists...rockets into that special corner of theater heaven where words shoot off like fireworks into dazzling patterns and hues." *—NY Times.* "An exhilarating, wicked...emotional terrorism." *—NY Newsday.* [2M, 2W] ISBN: 0-8222-1814-3

★ **FORCE CONTINUUM by Kia Corthron.** Tensions among black and white police officers and the neighborhoods they serve form the backdrop of this discomfiting look at life in the inner city. "The creator of this intense...new play is a singular voice among American playwrights...exceptionally eloquent..." *—NY Times.* "...a rich subject and a wise attitude." *—NY Post.* [6M, 2W, 1 boy] ISBN: 0-8222-1817-8

DRAMATISTS PLAY SERVICE, INC.
440 Park Avenue South, New York, NY 10016 212-683-8960 Fax 212-213-1539
postmaster@dramatists.com www.dramatists.com